Our architecture reflects us, as truly as a mirror . . .

LOUIS SULLIVAN

LOST CHICAGO

DAVID LOWE

AMERICAN LEGACY PRESS
NEW YORK

HALF-TITLE PAGE: Statue by Alfonso Iannelli for Frank Lloyd Wright's splendid, vanished 1914 creation, the Midway Gardens.

TITLE PAGE: The first University of Chicago, whose cornerstone was laid on July 4, 1857, stood at the corner of 34th Street and Cottage Grove Avenue. Constructed of cream-colored stone in what an early guidebook called "Norman or Romanesque style," it boasted a 156-foot tower. William W. Boyington was the architect. The building was damaged by fire in the 1880s and afterward demolished.

PAGE V: Door knob by Louis Sullivan for the Chicago Stock Exchange.

PAGE VI: A drawing of a wild onion plant, which in Indian is Chi-ca-gou, the probable source of the name of the city of Chicago.

A portion of this book has appeared in *Chicago History.*

The lines from "Abraham Lincoln Walks at Midnight" and "The Congo" are reprinted with permission of Macmillan Publishing Co., Inc. from *Collected Poems* by Vachel Lindsay, copyright 1914 by Macmillan Publishing Co., Inc., renewed 1942 by Elizabeth C. Lindsay. The lines from "Chicago" by Carl Sandburg are from *Chicago Poems*, published by Harcourt Brace Jovanovich, Inc. and reprinted here by permission. The lines from "Chicago" by Edgar Lee Masters are from *Starved Rock* and are reprinted by permission of Macmillan Publishing Company and Ellen C. Masters.

This 1985 edition is published by American Legacy Press, distributed by Crown Publishers, Inc., 225 Park Avenue South, New York, New York 10003, by arrangement with Houghton Mifflin Company.

Manufactured in the United States of America

Library of Congress Cataloging in Publication Data
Lowe, David, 1933-
    Lost Chicago.

    Reprint. Originally published: Boston : Houghton Mifflin, 1975.
    Bibliography: p.
    Includes index.
    1. Architecture—Illinois—Chicago. 2. Chicago (Il.)
—Buildings. I. Title.
[NA735.C4L68 1985]   720'.9773'11   84-28337
ISBN: 0-517-468883

h g f e

*For my father, who first took me
to Henrici's and the Union Stock Yards,
and my uncle, who won the American Derby
with Windy City*

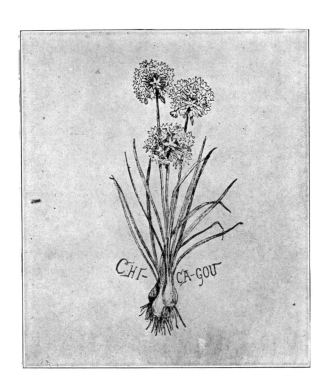

Acknowledgments

THE COMPLETION of this book was facilitated by a generous grant from Chicago's Graham Foundation for Advanced Studies in the Fine Arts. I would like to thank its director, Carter H. Manny, Jr., for his interest in this project.

* * *

While I was seeking photographs in archives and picture collections the following people were most helpful: Mary Frances Rhymer, curator of prints and photographs at the Chicago Historical Society, and her assistant, Julia Westerberg; Sally Forbes and Douglas Tunstell; William M. McLenahan, director, and Roy Forrey, staff writer, of the Commission on Chicago Historical and Architectural Landmarks; William S. Lieberman of the Museum of Modern Art; Byron C. Karzas; Oliver Jensen, editor in chief of *American Heritage;* Charles and Stewart Peacock of Spaulding's; Florene Marx Schoenborn; Muriel Morris Buttinger; the staff of Glessner House; Harry Price of Roosevelt University; Olga Valenta; Barbara Ballinger, head librarian, Oak Park Public Library; and Esther Bubley, whose camera is responsible for many of the excellent reproductions on these pages.

A special word of thanks goes to Annette Fern, reference librarian for architecture of the Art Institute of Chicago's Burnham Library, for her help both in collecting photographs and in tracking down the names of architects and the dates of the construction and destruction of buildings.

Many of the illustrations in this book are from the collections of photographers who generously granted me access to their files: Harold Allen, Barbara Crane, Jack Hedrich, Ralph Marlowe Line, and David Phillips.

Among those who provided information and help during the writing of the text were: Ferdinand Lundberg, who permitted me to draw on his experiences as a Chicago newspaperman in the 1920's; James T. Maher, who shared his knowledge of American music and architecture; John Maxon of the Art Institute of Chicago; Marion Knoblauch Franc of the Landmarks Preservation Council; Helen M. Brown; Coburn Britton; Florence Codman; Donald P. Gurney; Anita Loos; Brenda Niemand; and the staff of the Avery Architectural Library at Columbia University.

Joyce Hartman of Houghton Mifflin was not only the editor of this book, but at every turn helped with her knowledge and good taste.

Another whose good taste played a part in this project was Murray Belsky, editorial art director of the American Heritage Publishing Company.

Any book on Chicago must draw upon certain works: Alfred T. Andreas, *History of Chicago;* Carl W. Condit, *The Chicago School of Architecture;* John Drury, *Old Chicago Houses;* Paul Gilbert and Charles Bryson, *Chicago and its Makers;* Lloyd Lewis and Henry Justin Smith, *Chicago: The History of its Reputation;* Harriet Monroe, *John Wellborn Root;* Hugh Morrison, *Louis Sullivan: Prophet of Modern Architecture;* Bessie Louise Pierce, *A History of Chicago;* Ernest Poole, *Giants Gone;* Thomas Tallmadge, *Architecture in Old Chicago.*

I wish to express my gratitude to the New York Public Library, particularly to the staffs of the Art and the Local History and Genealogy rooms. I would like to thank the library too for the privilege of working in the Frederick Lewis Allen Room, where much of this labor was accomplished.

Finally, I salute the memory of one who will always be an inspiration to those who cherish Chicago, Richard Nickel, the photographer whose picture of the Stock Exchange graces the cover of this book and who was accidentally killed during the demolition of that building.

— D. L.

Contents

Preface

CHICAGO was always, for me, a magical city. When I was very young in the 1940s, the magic took the simple form of shopping with an aunt on State Street, luncheon beside the fountain of Marshall Field's Narcissus Room, and a tour of that perpetually wondrous Xanadu, Field's toy department. On very special occasions, I might be permitted to select a gift for myself, a stagecoach with four galloping horses or a PT boat which fired wooden projectiles. Sometimes, in the afternoon, we entered the exotic fantasy of the Oriental Theatre, and there amid the curious chinoiserie of its auditorium I sat entranced while, on the stage, the Mills Brothers sang "Paper Doll." Of all the city's richly varied movie palaces, the Oriental held first place in my heart, though it had stiff competition from the Paradise out west on Crawford Avenue, where Lorado Taft's statue of Apollo in his chariot raced tirelessly across a star-filled sky.

Later, Chicago's magic was enhanced by visits with my father to Henrici's on Randolph Street; amidst its Edwardian opulence of exuberantly carved wood, waving palms, and enormous paintings in gleaming golden frames, I was first introduced to such old-fashioned delicacies as finnan haddie and Pêche Melba. If we were going to the theatre, perhaps the Garrick almost across the street which my father continued to call by its original name, the Schiller, I might be told of that long-past glorious time when Chicago had boasted dozens of legitimate theatres and Sarah Bernhardt had announced that she preferred it to New York.

Both my father and my grandfather had worked in the Union Stock Yards, and no place was more magical than that vast congregation of bleating, grunting, lowing animals. The pens stretched for as far as the eye could see, the freight trains out of the West seemed endless, and the packing houses were entire towns unto themselves. Often I heard stories of the years when Nelson Morris, Gustavus Swift, and Philip D. Armour ruled the Yards, true princes of the blood.

But Chicago still had princely aspects in the late

1940s and the early '50s. There was the elegance of American Derby Day at Washington Park, conjuring up memories of that earlier Washington Park with its smart processions of broughams, landaus, and victorias. There was the sophisticated excitement of the arrival of the Twentieth Century Limited at the La Salle Street Station and the Hollywood-tinged glamour of the departure of the Chief and the Super Chief from the Dearborn. There was the sense of power, the summoning of the ghosts of Lincoln, William Jennings Bryan, and Franklin D. Roosevelt, during national political conventions. None was more dramatic than the one in 1952 when the lobbies of the Congress and the Blackstone and the Stevens — as we still called the Conrad Hilton — were jammed with delegates passionately split between Dwight Eisenhower and the hero of the heartland, Robert Alphonso Taft. There was the lingering '30s chic of the Chez Paree, with its dance bands and headliners such as Lena Horne. And always, at night, there was the shimmering fantasy of the Wrigley Building dominating Michigan Avenue, and, behind it, the Lindbergh Beacon atop the Palmolive Building, which gave to the Loop the sense of a perpetual première.

Indeed, the supreme magic of Chicago was always the sheer physical presence of the city, the unequaled splendor of its architecture. For me, growing up was coincidental with becoming aware of that architecture. As the names of its builders entered my consciousness — Le Baron Jenney, Dankmar Adler, Louis Sullivan, John Wellborn Root, Daniel Burnham, Henry Ives Cobb, William Holabird, Frank Lloyd Wright — I be-

gan to look about with interest and wonder and love. A walk through Chicago became a kind of pilgrimage to their creations: Adler and Sullivan's Auditorium and their Stock Exchange, Cobb's Potter Palmer castle and Federal Building, Burnham's Mecca, Wright's Francis Apartments, Holabird and Root's Diana Court. These were, in a very real sense, Chicago's true shrines, for here one felt that man had expressed his better nature, that he had, in some mysterious way, been in touch with a force greater than himself.

After college, when I moved away, every trip back to Chicago was a revelation of monuments fallen: the Mecca, the Palmer castle, the Garrick Theatre, the Federal Building, the long bar of the Auditorium, the Stock Exchange, Diana Court. Even lesser landmarks, the places that had given the city its special personality, were not spared: the Paradise Theatre, Henrici's, the Chez Paree, the Lindbergh Beacon, and, unbelievably, the Stock Yards themselves. Their owners had not saved them. City commissions had not saved them. They were an incomparable heritage mindlessly squandered, pieces of gold minted by the fathers and thrown away by the sons. I could not save them in their concrete form, but I was determined that somehow I would preserve their spirit. I would do it in the one way I could, by writing a book that would reveal them and their architectural predecessors in all their glory. Perhaps, by showing the splendor which has been lost, I might, in some small way, help to preserve that splendor not yet departed.

DAVID LOWE

LOST CHICAGO

The construction of the first Fort Dearborn in 1803 by Captain John Whistler marked the true founding of the city of Chicago. The center of the parade ground is now on the southwest corner of the Michigan Avenue bridge. The fort was burned the night of August 15, 1812, following the massacre of 52 settlers and soldiers.

I

The Island

IN THE BEGINNING there was only the great lake on the east and, to the west, the billowing sea of grass. Between them, a kind of island, the future site of Chicago was a damp place in which grew countless wild onions. Any understanding of the city, its grain elevators and packing houses, its rail yards and mail order business, its tall towers with their broad windows set to catch the morning sun, and its low earth-hugging prairie houses, must first take this into account.

Chicago is in the midst of sea-lanes as surely as Britain is. This fact has made everything else possible. The level sea of grass and water about it gave impetus to its architects to raise unchallenged mountains from whose tops they could sight across a continent and to build pattern-shattering houses, as sheltering as cottages on the edge of a stormy ocean. For Chicago is not inland. Springfield, Massachusetts, is inland; Harrisburg, Pennsylvania, is inland; Chicago is not. To the New Englanders and New Yorkers who

journeyed out in the nineteenth century it seemed inland; seemed so because they had traveled across western New York and Ohio and Michigan and Indiana to get there. But it cannot be called inland unless one considers Naples on the Tyrrhenian and Venice on the Adriatic Sea inland. Those who have witnessed the twelve-foot breakers crashing along the lake and beheld the waves of snow on the great plain stretching limitless to the Arctic know that it is a city on an island between two seas.

There are places that have the good fortune to have their beginnings attended by romance. Rome, with its legend of Romulus and Remus, and New York, with its purchase by Peter Minuit for the equivalent of $24, are two. Philadelphia's beginnings are without romance, as are Washington's. Chicago's are rife with it. The very words most commonly associated with the city's birth, *coureurs de bois,* are redolent of the splash of a paddle upon a crystal lake, of men in buckskin, of afternoon shadows slanting through a

1

virgin wood. Among the Europeans who came to this continent, the French were the first to see the site of Chicago. They did not discover it; it was not lost. For centuries Miamis and Illinois and Potawatomis and Ottawas and Chippewas had roamed over it, gathering there to trade pelts for corn, feathers for flint. And it was the Indians who named this ground of meeting and passage. They called it "Chi-ca-gou," the Place of the Wild Onion.

The recorded history of Chicago begins with two extraordinary Frenchmen, Jacques Marquette, a Jesuit priest from Laon in Picardy, and Louis Jolliet, native of Quebec, fur trader, discoverer, seeker after copper. In 1673, on their way back to Green Bay following their exploration of the Mississippi, Marquette and Jolliet crossed the Chicago portage. They found the countryside along the Illinois River rich and full of promise. Father Marquette wrote in his diary:

We have seen nothing like this river that we enter, as regards its fertility of soil, its prairies and woods; its cattle, elk, deer, wildcats, bustards, swans, ducks, parroquets, and even beaver.

This was variety enough to attract any hunter of animals, but Marquette was a hunter of souls, and the next winter, in December of 1674, he returned to Chicago to preach the gospel to the Indians, thus becoming the city's patron, its first romantic legend, its Romulus. Marquette built a shelter, "une cabannez," which in the patois of the *coureurs de bois* meant either a hut or a wigwam. Most likely it was a hut made in the French fashion of upright poles sunk in the ground, chinked and plastered over with clay and roofed with other poles over which was laid bark or hides.

For almost a hundred years after this, during the long reign of Louis XIV and of his great-grandson, Louis XV, the country of the Illinois would be ruled from Versailles; its loss to the English would later be an important factor in the decision of Louis XV's grandson, Louis XVI, to help the American colonies in their revolution. It was a part of that vibrant French world which stretched from the Strait of Belle Isle on Canada's far Atlantic coast, through Quebec and Montreal, and down the Mississippi past Dubuque and St. Louis to New Orleans.

Other Frenchmen came after Marquette: priests and hunters and traders and trappers. But it is Robert Cavelier, Sieur de La Salle, who is remembered above all. It was La Salle who claimed what became Louisiana for the French, pushed for the establishment of a great city at the mouth of the Father of Waters, built a fort at Starved Rock overlooking the Illinois River. And it was La Salle who, sometime around 1681, began using the word Chi-ca-gou to indicate specifically the site of the present city rather than the whole region.

The French era in Chicago ended in 1759 with the defeat of Montcalm by Wolfe upon Quebec's Plains of Abraham. But the influence of the French did not end. Inspecting the territory in 1766, an English officer, Captain Harry Gordon, reported back to his superior, General Thomas Gage, that the French were carrying on trade "all around . . . by Land and Water." Once the American Revolution had begun, this was a situation which the British could not tolerate. A prime object of their suspicion was Jean Baptiste Point Sable, a native of Santo Domingo, born of a French father and a black slave mother, who was described as "a handsome negro (well educated and settled in Eschecagou), but much in the French interest." Point Sable was not only handsome and educated, he was a highly successful trader possessing a mill, numerous outbuildings, in addition to a dwelling built in the manner of those found in all the French settlements of the mid-American continent — logs of modest diameter set upright, fastened at their top with a horizontal timber, and the whole structure surrounded by a porch. In 1779 he was arrested by the British and sent to Mackinac Island for the duration. Point Sable's house really marks the beginning of permanent settlement in Chicago. After the Revolution, he would return and then, at the end of the eighteenth century, sell his house to a French trader named Le Mai, who would in turn sell it to John Kinzie, who bore the first important non-Gallic name in the city's history.

But before that, before names such as Kinzie with all its connotations of the Yankee world of serious sabbaths and steady industry could come to Chicago, there had to be a revolution. Chicago's early days are marked by the influence of unseen battles in distant places. The Plains of Abraham had made it British; now Yorktown made it American. President Washington, aware of its strategic location at the head of the water routes leading into the heart of the continent, wanted to build a fort there. But it was the

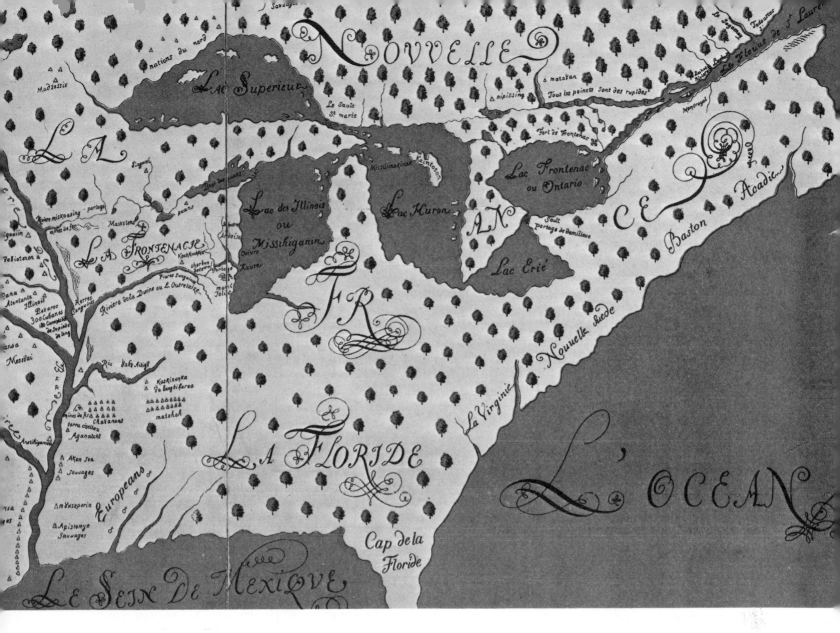

Details of two maps from the French era of America's heartland. *Above:* This is believed to be the map that Louis Jolliet drew in 1674, the year after he and Jacques Marquette crossed the Chicago portage. The Illinois River is here called the Outrelaize. *Right:* This map of 1703, drawn by Louis Armand de Lom d'Arce, Baron de La Hontan, gives a fairly accurate picture of the region at the beginning of the eighteenth century. At this time "Chicago" was spelled in a variety of ways.

Louisiana Purchase of 1803 that made the fort a necessity. In July of that year, Captain John Whistler, under orders from General Henry Dearborn of the War Department, came to Chicago to build it. Years later, in London, the painter James McNeill Whistler was asked by a Chicagoan if he had ever been to the city. "No," Whistler replied, "but my grandfather founded the place."

Captain Whistler built Fort Dearborn near what is now Michigan Avenue on the south side of the Chicago River. It was constructed in the American style, with the logs laid horizontally one on top of another, locked at the corners by notches and the spaces between chinked with a mixture of clay, straw, and moss. It was an impressive structure. There were storehouses, a powder magazine, a blockhouse, quarters for a modest garrison of some seventy officers and men. It was the beginning of civic architecture in Chicago, the first public building, the core of the future city. In an attempt to wean the rich trade with the Indians away from the British, there was also a government factory or trading house. And now, mingling with those named Bourbonne and Ouilmette (which transmogrified to Wilmette would give its bearer a kind of immortality), appeared men called Hayward and Varnum and Irwin, men who came overland from the former English colonies of the Atlantic seaboard rather than down the lakes from Montreal and Quebec. None was more typical of these than John Kinzie, who arrived in the spring of 1804. Establishing himself opposite the fort on the north bank of the river, he was soon trading with the Indians, equipping trappers, supplying the garrison, and doing a considerable business in articles of silver he himself made. Within five years of the construction of Fort Dearborn, the population of Chicago, not counting the garrison, had reached the impressive total of forty souls.

For the first eight or nine years after the fort was built all went smoothly, almost dully. The whole surrounding country was still prairie, with the quiet routine of the settlement broken only by the fur traders who headed out to the beaver country in autumn and came back with their pelts in the spring. Now and then there would be the supreme excitement of a wolf hunt when one of the numerous packs sloped too near. Chicago seemed destined to grow gradually outward, ring upon ring, like a maturing tree, like Louisville or St. Louis or Indianapolis. But that was never the

style of the place of the wild onion. It had always had a flare for the dramatic, an undeniable rendezvous with history.

In Europe, Napoleon and the English were engaged in a vast, titanic struggle for control of the continent, and, in a sense, for control of the world. The United States had watched the battles — Marengo, Trafalgar, Austerlitz — from the sidelines, but there was no doubt where the nation's sympathies lay. There was a profound sense of gratitude for French help in the Revolution, a still-bitter hatred of the English, and a strong sentiment for annexing Canada. In 1812 President Madison finally declared war on England. It was not a wise move. The British won victory after victory and encouraged the Indians, with promises of a return of their western lands, to attack American settlements. Chicago was particularly vulnerable, and word came on August 9, 1812, to evacuate Fort Dearborn. Plans were made as quickly as possible, but by the time the evacuation began on the fifteenth, there were some 500 Potawatomi warriors in the vicinity. It was a tiny procession that left the stockade. The garrison of fifty-five regulars, a militia company of twelve citizens and, loaded into two wagons pulled by oxen, nine women and eighteen children. They counted on their consistently friendly relations with the Indians to protect them.

The column had not proceeded more than a mile and a half when the warriors attacked. "The troops behaved most gallantly. They were but a handful," Margaret Helm, one of the women, wrote later. "In the meantime a horrible scene was enacted. One young savage, climbing into the baggage-wagon containing the children of the white families tomahawked nearly all of them." When the battle was over, twenty-six regulars, all of the militia, two women, and twelve children were dead. Of those captured, some were tortured to death on the shore of Lake Michigan; others perished as captives. A few eventually escaped — among them the Kinzies. There, on that bright August morning, between the great lake and the sea of grass, was born the legend of the Fort Dearborn massacre.

After plundering the fort, the Indians set it afire, and soon only the damaged powder magazine remained to proclaim the United States' western empire. Now only a few French-Canadian traders or British-paid Indian war parties on their way to attack American settlements passed the still-unburied bodies of the slain. It was a precarious moment in the history of Chicago. The region might well have remained British, or perhaps no new settlement, no fresh growth of village would have sprung up at the portage. But the peace treaty of 1815 once more returned the site to the United States and the importance of the island between the two seas was not forgotten. In 1816 the order went out from Washington to build a new Fort Dearborn. There was one feature of the second fort that could be called an attempt at serious architecture, and this was its two-story porches. These verandahs with their slender wooden columns were a rustic echo of the splendid Federal style which had swept all before it along the Atlantic seaboard. These columns were Chicago's first feeble stirrings of architectural consciousness, its primitive copy of the elegant pilasters with which Samuel McIntire was adorning the houses of Salem's Chestnut Street.

The same year that the second fort was built, John Kinzie returned with his family and took up residence in his old cabin. Other survivors returned too, such as the Ouilmettes; and new ones came. There was fiddle-playing Mark Beaubien, who, by building two inns, the Eagle Exchange, near what is now the northeast corner of Randolph and Market Streets, and the Sauganash, at the corner of Lake and Market, became the godfather of Chicago's grand hotels. There were also more and more Yankees, among them Gurdon S. Hubbard, a native of Windsor, Vermont,

who was an agent for John Jacob Astor's American Fur Company. In time he would become one of the town's first packers and would make a fortune in real estate. But Hubbard has another claim to remembrance, for he was the man who cleared a trail from Danville, Illinois, north to Chicago. It was first called Hubbard's Trail, then State Road, and later still, State Street.

There were already, for the observant, prophetic signs pointing toward the urban magnificence which the words "State Street," "Michigan Avenue," and "Lake Shore Drive" would one day connote. Illinois had been admitted to the Union in 1818, and Chicago's trade with the region's growing population was booming. There was even talk of a canal linking the Great Lakes with the Mississippi, which would make the Place of the Wild Onion the key to unlocking the riches of the North American continent. No one saw these signs more clearly than the pioneer geologist Henry Schoolcraft:

The country around Chicago is the most fertile and beautiful that can be imagined . . . to the ordinary advantages of an agricultural marketing town, it must, hereafter, add that of a depot, for inland commerce, between the northern and southern sections of the Union, and a great thoroughfare for strangers, merchants and travelers.

Buildings for a City

Henry James, writing to his brother William, expressed the excitement he felt on being in Rome: "In the course of four or five hours I traversed almost the whole of Rome and got a glimpse of everything — the Forum, the Coliseum (stupendissimo!), the Pantheon, the Capitol . . ." The great public buildings of a city should indeed stir us, for they are the true treasuries of a people's experience. Here famous men and women acted and spoke; here took place those events that affected the course of a nation's history. The survival of such buildings help us, in a very real way, to draw near those people and those events. It is a dead imagination that is not quickened by being told: "Lincoln spoke here" or "This was the scene of Clarence Darrow's last trial." Chicago has been prodigal in its destruction of its civic structures. The sacking of the first Fort Dearborn and the fire of 1871 robbed the city of much of its historical architectural heritage, but later public buildings have been casually obliterated with scarcely a pause to consider their significance.

A second **Fort Dearborn** (*below*) was constructed in 1816 under the direction of Captain Hezekiah Bradley. In her book, *Wau-Bun, The Early Day in the North-West,* Juliette Kinzie remembered: "The fort was enclosed with high pickets, with bastions at alternate angles." In this 1856 view by the pioneer Chicago photographer Alexander Hesler, the fort has lost both pickets and bastions, but its officers' and enlisted men's quarters are still standing. They were demolished the next year.

The first **Court House** in Chicago (*above*), built in 1835.
It stood at the corner of Clark and Randolph Streets.

The growing self-assurance of Chicago is reflected in the handsome second Court
House (*below*) designed in 1853 by the city's first architect, John Van Osdel. This
1855 daguerreotype shows the Montgomery and Emmett Guards drawn up to hear
a Fourth of July oration by Mayor John Wentworth. The structure occupied the
center of the block bounded by La Salle, Clark, Randolph, and Washington Streets,
still the site of Chicago's government buildings. It was here that Abraham Lincoln's
body lay in state, and it was the Court House bell which sounded the alarm for the
Great Chicago Fire until the building itself was consumed in the holocaust.

After the fire, Chicago sought to assert its recovery by raising a city hall to rival the costly municipal edifices being built in Philadelphia and elsewhere. In terms of both lavishness and size, Chicago's City and County Building was second to none. The work principally of James J. Egan, the county architect, the vast structure took nearly a dozen years to build and did not open until 1885. Many were impressed by it. "The heart and center of Chicago is the huge pile of masonry which reminds the visitor by its polished granite pillars and general massive and somber grandeur of the cathedrals and palaces of St. Petersburg," the English writer William T. Stead observed in *If Christ Came to Chicago!* The city's aldermen defended the building's $5 million cost by saying that it had been built for the ages. Egan's confection was pulled down in 1906–08.

In the last decade of the nineteenth century, Chicago felt itself a kind of second capital of the United States, and it was not unusual to hear proposals that it supersede Washington. In keeping with its growing importance, the federal government decided to honor the city with a building that would be its administrative center for the Midwest. Henry Ives Cobb, the architect of the Potter Palmer mansion, brilliantly reflected the city's pride with his classical dome-crowned edifice. In one of its courtrooms, Judge Kenesaw Mountain Landis fined the Standard Oil Company $29 million; in another, Al Capone was sentenced to a penitentiary for income tax evasion. The Federal Building, the most notable example of civic architecture in Chicago, was wantonly demolished in 1965–66.

Chicago's early interest in painting resulted in the Art Institute on Michigan Avenue (*at right in the photograph above*), one of the most successful Romanesque designs by the internationally known architects Daniel Burnham and John Wellborn Root. After its opening in 1885, it was the scene of trail-blazing exhibitions of the work of the French Impressionists. When the Art Institute moved across Michigan Avenue in the 1890s, its old home became the august Chicago Club. The building collapsed in 1929 during remodeling. The building on the left — still standing today — is the Fine Arts, by Solon S. Beman; it was the focus of the city's creative life, where Little Theatre began in America and where, before the First World War, Margaret Anderson published *The Little Review*.

One of the city's most exotic structures, the Chicago Board of Trade Building of 1885 (*right, above*), was the work of William W. Boyington, designer of the famed Water Tower. The building, at the head of La Salle Street, was the focus of Frank Norris' powerful novel *The Pit,* and its trading room (*right, below*), where wheat, corn, and other grain were bought and sold, was vividly described by him: "It was a vast enclosure lighted on either side by great windows of coloured glass . . . a row of tables, laden with neatly arranged paper bags half full of samples of grains, stretched along the east wall. . . . The center of the floor was occupied by the pit." Boyington's building was replaced by the present Board of Trade quarters in the late 1920s.

The astonishing growth of Chicago just forty years after the construction of the
second Fort Dearborn is revealed in this photograph of 1858 looking southeast from
the corner of Washington and La Salle Streets. The church is the First Baptist,
built in 1853; the architect is unknown. In 1864, it was purchased by the Second
Baptist congregation and moved across the river to the corner of Monroe and
Morgan Streets where it survived well into the twentieth century. Behind the church
can be seen a row of Greek Revival houses of the type that gave to early Chicago
the air of a New England village.

II

Time of the Temple

THE 1830s MARKED an important phase in the development of Chicago, for in that decade the once-modest village moved swiftly toward cityhood. In 1830 Chicago was plotted and surveyed, and the following year it was designated the seat of the new Cook County, a name honoring Illinois's first attorney general, one Daniel P. Cook, who most likely never set foot in the place which would confer upon him his only lasting fame. Soon a post office was established, a lighthouse and sawmill built, and the first bridge — consisting of floating logs — was stretched across the Chicago River at what is now Randolph Street. In 1833 Chicago was incorporated as a town. Charles Joseph Latrobe, a celebrated English visitor to America in these years, saw Chicago in the eighteen thirties and recorded in his *Rambler in North America:* "I have been in many odd assemblages of my species, but in few, if any, of an equally singular character as with that in the midst of which we spent a week at Chicago . . ." It seems that they were already doing things on Hubbard's Trail that they didn't do on Broadway.

The village was teeming with fur traders, land speculators, new immigrants, gamblers, horse thieves, Indians, and soldiers. The last two, however, were about to depart the scene. During 1831 and 1832, the settlers had been frightened by reports of Indian outrages, mostly the work of the Sauk and Fox tribes led by the powerful chief Black Hawk. After Black Hawk's defeat, the United States government decided to expel all Indians from the fertile, long-coveted region stretching from the southern half of Lake Michigan to the Mississippi. So in 1835, the Potawatomi, some 5000 in number, gathered in Chicago for the last time to receive their government annuities, bid farewell to their old hunting grounds, and depart for their new homes in the West. The early Chicago historian John Dean Caton was present, and has left a vivid account of that melancholy goodbye.

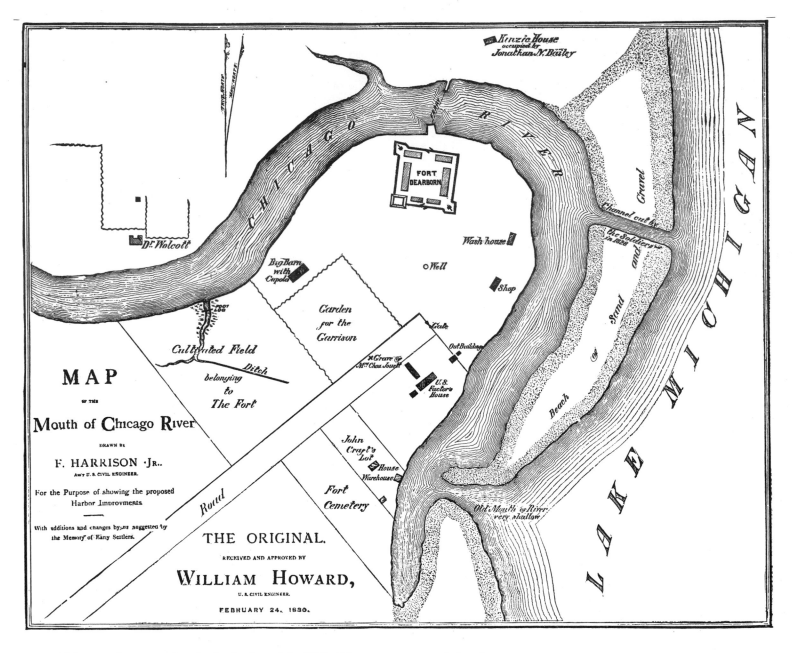

Chicago as it appeared at the beginning of the 1830s. The map was commissioned by the United States government so that plans could be made for improving the city's harbor.

They assembled at the council-house, near where the Lake House now stands, on the north side of the river. All were entirely naked, except for a strip of cloth around the loins. Their bodies were covered all over with a great variety of brilliant paints . . . The long, coarse, black hair was gathered into scalp-locks on the tops of their heads, and decorated with a profusion of hawk's and eagle's feathers . . . They advanced, not with a regular march, but a continued dance.

Thus the Indian danced out of Chicago's history. With the Red Man no longer a threat, Fort Dearborn itself was evacuated in 1836, and slowly slipped into oblivion until its last vestiges disappeared in the great fire.

The 1830s were a fortuitous moment to begin the construction of a city, for America had embraced a new architecture. If the first century and a half of Chicago's history can be termed the period of the cabin and the fort, the next twenty-five years may be called the time of the temple. After the Federal style with its reflection of the work of the brothers Adam, its avid admiration of the formal squares and crescents of English cities such as Bath and London, America had found another model: Greece. There were both aesthetic and political reasons for this change. In the first place, the War of 1812, with the burning of the President's house and the Capitol, had stirred up violent anti-British sentiment in the United States. Second, the Greek War of Independence of the 1820s against the Turks had deeply aroused Americans who identified with ancient Greece's republican traditions. In a thousand villages with names such as Athens and Corinth and Sparta, the citizens of the new republic paid tribute to the old.

Aesthetically, the tradition began with a book, *The Antiquities of Athens,* by two Englishmen, James Stuart and Nicholas Revett, the first volume of which was published in London in 1762. By 1770 a copy had found its way to the Library Company of Philadelphia where it was subsequently studied by Benjamin Latrobe, the second architect of the Capitol, who introduced the Greek Revival style into the United States, and other architects of the nation's early years such as William Strickland, Thomas U. Walter, and Robert Mills. It was not long before illustrated manuals by builders such as John Haviland, Asher Benjamin, and John Hall had made it possible for any competent carpenter to produce structures with all the trappings of Greek temples: fluted and plain columns, capitals of every order, pediments, pilasters, fasciae, and metopes. And soon the style, in stone or adapted to brick and wood, swept the country from Montpelier, Vermont, to Frankfort, Kentucky.

It was an ideal style for a city only a day or two by schooner away from the seemingly inexhaustible Michigan forests of white pine, one of the finest woods in the world. Here were millions of growing columns, perfectly straight, selling for a mere $20 per thousand board feet. Brick was used for the larger buildings, but for the great bulk of Chicago's new structures, pine was the marble.

The special glory of the Greek Revival style, as practiced in the United States, was that it was readily adaptable to almost every need. When it came to domestic architecture, it stretched to any size, from modest story-and-a-half cottages with pilasters at the corners and simple Greek-type moldings, to columned mansions such as one built in 1836 by Virginian Archibald Clybourne, Chicago's first constable. Undoubtedly one of the supreme examples of domestic Greek Revival architecture was the house that Eli B. Williams, registrar of the United States Land Office, erected at the southeast corner of Monroe and Wabash. With its splendid portico of six Doric columns and its fine proportions, the Williams house was a temple worthy of the classical towns of New York and New England.

The style served just as well for churches and schools, shops and offices, hotels and public buildings. Thus it was inevitable that Chicago's first Court House, built in 1835 at the corner of the Public Square at Clark and Randolph Streets, should have been a templelike rectangular brick building ennobled by a free-standing portico of four wooden Doric columns. The Greek Revival was evident in the Saloon Building at the southwest corner of Lake and Clark Streets, the Faneuil Hall of the early city where, in 1837, the young Stephen A. Douglas captured Chicago's collective heart. It was the manner of the three-story Bank of Illinois on the corner of South Water and La Salle Streets and of the Lake House, the first hotel in town to boast a French chef and a printed menu.

Chicago had need of a vast variety of buildings, for the 1830s were boom times in the old Northwest. It was a period of one of the greatest migrations in the history of mankind, a migration which ranks with the movement of the Huns into Europe and of the German tribes south into Italy and Spain. At the beginning of the decade the population of Chicago numbered one hundred; by the end it was more than 4000. The key factor in the city's spectacular growth was the completion, in 1825, of the Erie Canal, linking the Great Lakes with the sea and making it possible for the traveler to move by water from the Atlantic coast to Illinois, Minnesota, and Wisconsin. Suddenly, from being almost deserted, the Chicago lake front became a forest of masts, and by 1843 the city was clearing some 700 vessels a year.

Indeed, Chicago was so packed with newcomers, with Yankee settlers, with businessmen, with laborers who had come to work on the canal that was being built to link Lake Michigan and the Mississippi, with speculators and passers-through that it was almost impossible to shelter them. If licensing had been in effect, half the dwellings in town would have qualified as boardinghouses. In 1835 more than 80 percent of the population of Chicago had been there less than a year. Charles Butler, a New York real estate broker and railroad promoter, was astonished by what he saw:

Emigrants were coming in almost every day in wagons of various forms and in many instances families were living in their covered wagons while arrangements were made for putting up shelter for them. It was no uncommon thing for a house such as would answer the purpose for the time being to be put up in a few days.

This need to erect a house in a few days resulted in the first example of that extraordinary inventiveness which Chicago was to display throughout the last two thirds of the nineteenth century. No city in the East had grown as rapidly as this, and wooden buildings had continued to be "framed" with heavy, slow, expensive post construction, just as they had been in medieval England. A chance to break away from this tedious and wasteful method was made possible by the circular steam-driven saw which permitted lumber to be cut into much smaller units, into two-by-fours and two-by-twelves and one-by-tens. Man was thus ready for one of those seminal inventions as important as the arch and the dome. Using these new cuts, Chicago builders began putting up light,

strong, and inexpensive "balloon frames." The invention was not only important in itself, but it revealed a new cast of mind, the mind of the prairie, a mind not looking back across the sea to castles and cathedrals, but looking forward to a new world. Here we now stood, in our own land.

One man, more than any other, symbolizes the boomtown of the '30s. William Butler Ogden's introduction to Chicago certainly did not portend a love affair. When he came out in 1835 from his native New York State it was to attempt to save the family fortune from what he considered the rash investment of a rich brother-in-law. The rash investment was a 182-acre tract close to the river on the north side. Anxious to salvage what he could of the $100,000 purchase price, Ogden ordered the entire parcel auctioned off at once. But then something surprising happened. The $100,000 had been retrieved by the time only a third of the land had been sold. Ogden halted the auction and decided to take a closer look at this curious collection of human beings gathered on Lake Michigan's western shore.

Ogden not only looked, he fell in love with Chicago. And his passion was not blind. Within two years the newcomer had made a fortune in real estate, and when, in 1837, Chicago was chartered as a city, William Ogden became its first mayor. Here was a new type of Chicagoan totally different from the voyageurs and the traders, the Kinzies and the Ouilmettes. Here was a man on a new scale, a businessman with a vision. That vision was to make the city the hub of the heartland, to bring every farm in the Midwest, every ear of corn, every grain of wheat, every hog and steer, within easy reach. But that would take time. Before then, he would give Chicago a very special gift: its first architect.

Ogden had met John Van Osdel in New York, and after he became mayor he sent for him to build a house worthy of this new civic dignity. Van Osdel arrived, not only with the plans for Chicago's first architect-designed dwelling, but with the necessary windows, stair rails, and trimmings as well. The architect of William Ogden's house was the supreme builder of Greek Revival Chicago. He was also one of those completely sympathetic people: an editor of the *American Mechanic*, which later became the *Scientific American*, a dedicated Garrisonian Abolitionist, and a man of great social charm. From his office on Clark Street flowed an almost endless stream of houses, hotels, and public buildings. He was responsible for the new Court House, the dedication of which was marked by a proud procession half a mile in length that included all the grandees of the burgeoning city: the military and fire companies, members of the Mechanics Institute, the political clubs, the Free Masons and the Odd Fellows. Three stories in height, crowned by a tall cupola, the Court House cost more than $100,000 but the good citizens felt that it was worth it, for the edifice was a proclamation that Chicago must now be taken seriously.

Of all of Van Osdel's buildings of this period, however, none is more significant than the emperor of early Chicago hostelries, the Tremont House, which he constructed in 1850 on the southeast corner of Lake and Dearborn Streets. The first Tremont House, built in the 1830s, had been a simple wooden structure, not very different from the city's old inns where accommodations had often been merely a mat on the floor. Van Osdel's hotel changed all that forever. "The Tremont House has precedence of all others," the paper *Gem of the Prairie* boasted in January 1851. "It is one of the chief ornaments of the city. . . . The house is five and a half stories high and its internal arrangements, including furniture and decorations, are all in the highest style of art, and of the class denominated princely." The significant word here is "princely," for Chicago was already intent upon creating hotels where every man was a king; it is but a step from the Tremont's marble mantels and rosewood furniture to the crystal-filled ballrooms of the great hotels of the post-fire years. In the Tremont's public rooms the early Chambers of Commerce met, business was transacted in its lobby, and, in time, history would be made from its balconies.

Van Osdel was as capable of turning out a playhouse as a hotel or a court house, and in 1851 he built a splendid one for John B. Rice, the father of the Chicago theatre. The settlement already had a not inconsiderable history of entertainment. In its very first year as a city, Harry Isherwood, a member of the theatrical firm of Isherwood and McKenzie, came from the East and put on plays in the old Sauganash Hotel. Soon the city had a real playhouse, a room thirty feet wide and eighty feet long, located on Dearborn Street and proudly calling itself the Chicago Theatre. There, in 1838, a troupe headed by Joseph Jefferson, Sr., came to delight one and all with *She Stoops to Conquer, The Magpie and the Maid,* and

something called *The Turn Out, or the Enraged Politician.* Among the players was a nine-year-old boy, Joseph Jefferson, Jr., who was to become nationally famous in the role of Rip Van Winkle. Jefferson vividly recalled his first impression of the city:

. . . off we go ashore and walk through the busy little town, busy even then, people hurrying to and fro, frame buildings going up, board sidewalks going down, new hotels, new churches, new theaters, everything new. Saw and hammer — saw! saw! bang! bang! — look out for the drays! — bright and muddy streets, gaudy-colored calicos, blue and red flannels and striped ticking hanging outside the drygoods store, bar-rooms, real-estate offices, attorneys-at-law . . .

The theatre, he remembered, had a drop curtain with "a medallion of Shakespeare, suffering from a severe pain in his stomach, over the center, with 'One touch of nature makes the whole world kin' written under him."

Delight in diversion was characteristic of Chicago from its infancy. At a period when the Midwest was being thickly settled with communities dedicated to high-mindedness rather than to high-living — Oberlin in Ohio, New Harmony in Indiana, Bishop Hill in Illinois — Chicago came down strongly on the side of having a good time. It was a city where, in the 1840s and '50s, a "grocery" meant an establishment that sold liquor as well as foodstuffs, and many of them managed to find room for a roulette wheel as well. Of course there were those who objected to all this frivolity. But when, on April 21, 1855, a number of persons were put on trial for violating Sunday closing laws, a riot ensued in which several policemen were injured. That same year a referendum was held on the question of prohibiting the sale of liquor. The citizens made it emphatically clear where they stood — or staggered. The results: For the prohibition, 2784; against 4093.

Yet the city's churches prospered too. When Father John St. Cyr arrived in 1833 to minister to Chicago's thirty-six Catholic families, he took one look at the log cabin which was to be his chapel and decided to build something more impressive. What he got was better, though by no stretch of the imagination could it be called splendid. St. Mary's, on the corner of State and Lake Streets, was an unplastered roughboard structure 36 feet long and 24 feet wide, in which a simple table served as the altar. Its total cost was $400. The next year the Presbyterians and Baptists built churches.

It was left to the Episcopalians, though, to construct Chicago's first important church building. They had staked out a parish in the midst of the wealthy residential sections of the North Side, with no less a personage for senior warden than John H. Kinzie, son of the trader who had settled beside Fort Dearborn. When, in 1837, they consecrated their new St. James Church on the corner of Cass and Illinois Streets, it was clear that they had chosen their location astutely. A faintly Gothic building, St. James had the distinction of being the first brick church in town; it also had the first tower as well as the first organ.

If men such as William Ogden were settling in this new city on the island between the lake and the prairie, if actors readily found audiences there, if the population was approaching 20,000, if its large hotels were filled, if domes and towers were rising above the cottonwoods, it was because of commerce. And if commerce was increasing at a fantastic rate, it was because of the island's extraordinary location. No one saw this more clearly than Margaret Fuller, the trancendentalist friend of Emerson and Hawthorne's, who arrived in 1843:

There can be no two places in the world more completely thoroughfares than this place and Buffalo. They are the two correspondent valves that open and shut all the time, as the life-blood rushes from east to west, and back again from west to east.

The first artery of this gigantic circulatory system was the Erie Canal; the second was the Illinois and Michigan Canal — linking the lakes with the tributaries of the Mississippi and thus with the Gulf of Mexico. One hears time and again of the Suez and Panama canals, but this canal, first prophesied by Jolliet, had effects as profound as either of those. Now it was possible to go by water from New York to New Orleans, and Chicago was the system's heart. The position of the island had been assured when it was a portage; it was now a port; it would one day, for the same reasons, become a harbor for trains. Men noticed the island's fortuitous location, and men, extraordinary men, built Chicago, such men as built no other American city. One can easily write a book called "Makers of Chicago," but it would be difficult

to write a "Makers of New York" or "Makers of Boston." And now one of the giants appeared.

In 1832 in the Blue Ridge Mountains of Virginia, a young inventor had brought forth a clumsy contraption of wood and iron pulled by four horses. But the ungainly contrivance could do something unheard of, something as revolutionary as James Hargreaves' spinning jenny or Eli Whitney's cotton gin: it could cut six acres of wheat in less time than it took six men to do it by hand. Cyrus McCormick began offering his machines for sale, and canny Scot that he was, he noticed that more and more of his orders came from the new lands of the West, from Illinois, Iowa, and Indiana. Virginia was inconveniently far from these markets and, looking for a better location for the factory he hoped to build, McCormick decided upon Chicago. There, in the autumn of 1847, in partnership with Charles M. Gray, who already had a reputation for his fine grain cradles and scythes, and with backing from the ever-alert William Ogden, Cyrus McCormick began the manufacture of his reapers.

If Eli Whitney is credited with the creation of the cotton kingdom, then it is not too much to say that Cyrus McCormick created the kingdom of wheat, for the Old Northwest was, in the eighteen forties and fifties, a one-crop region, and wheat was that one crop. Chicago, almost exclusively, was its port of exit. In 1843, the city had sent 700,000 bushels to the eastern markets; by 1847, when McCormick's reapers had begun to make an impact, it sent 2,000,000.

Carl Sandburg was one day to stamp Chicago indelibly as the "Stacker of Wheat" and the "Hog Butcher for the World." Now, in the Greek Revival city of the '40s and '50s, the foundations of the second of these vast enterprises were also laid. The slaughtering of livestock was nothing new for the city. Gurdon Hubbard had begun it in the '20s, and there had been Mark and John Noble, and Archibald Clybourne, official butcher to the soldiers at Fort Dearborn, and George Dole, who in 1833 had slaughtered a number of cattle, packed the beef in barrels, and shipped it to Detroit. But all of this was on a small scale, comparable to Chicago's agricultural-implement manufacturing before the advent of Cyrus McCormick. It took a man with a special genius to make it into a great enterprise. That man, Nelson Morris, who arrived in 1852 as a boy of fifteen, represented a new addition to the lifeblood of the city.

He was German and Jewish, from Franconia, and somehow in the villages where he and his father bought and sold cattle, he had heard of Chicago — a name already synonymous with opportunity. The hopeful dream of millions in the nineteenth century drew him to this new land.

Alone, at the age of twelve, Morris arrived in Philadelphia, almost penniless and with little formal education. But it was not of the East he had heard, but of the West, and slowly over a period of three years he worked his way there, one month as a farm laborer, the next as a charcoal burner, earning his passage on the Erie Canal to Buffalo and on a Great Lakes freighter to Michigan City, Indiana, and then walking the rest of the way to Chicago. His long journey had tutored him well in English, and he got a job with John B. Sherman, who had founded the city's first stock yards at Ogden Avenue and Madison Street. His salary was five dollars a month, but he knew cattle and soon had a reputation as the smartest buyer in the yards. Before long he had his own packing company. Morris pioneered the idea of using "everything but the squeal" to make margarine and buttons and glue and fertilizer and isinglass, pioneered the idea of refrigerator boxcars, pioneered the idea of assembly-line production. Again, as it was with McCormick's harvester works, it was the location of the island that made it all possible. Here the cattle could be driven overland from the farms of the heartland and the ranches of the West, slaughtered, and then shipped by water to the markets of the East. At first it was land and water; later it would be the rails, but always everything was possible because of the invisible but compelling travel-lanes of the continent.

The endpapers of this volume reproduce a crayon drawing, a bird's-eye view from Lake Michigan; executed in 1853, the year after Nelson Morris arrived in Chicago, it shows the Greek Revival city in all its magnificence. It is stunning in its architectural purity. It might be Charleston or Boston of the Federal period or the port of New York when Trinity Church dominated the skyline. But it is Chicago, a Chicago that it is now difficult to believe ever existed, a Chicago, in its own way, as rare and exotic and fabulous as medieval Paris or pre-fire London. It is a city of ample squares and tree-lined streets, of tall-spired churches that look as though they had been built in New England, a city dominated by Van Osdel's proud classical Court House. In the foreground, on track laid on pilings along the lakeshore, a smoke-belching train moves north. The train is important. It will bring new life, new business, new people, new money, but it will also destroy the green and white Greek Revival city.

Residences

Nigel Nicolson, the English writer, makes an interesting argument for preserving old houses in the introduction to his *Great Houses of Britain:* "Apart from emphasizing the architectural inventiveness of the British, these houses also illustrate how our ancestors lived and, to some extent, how they thought." The systematic destruction over the past fifty years of America's old residences — great houses, modest dwellings, and apartment buildings — has been one of the major factors in the architectural impoverishment of our cities. This vandalism has also created an almost insuperable barrier to a full understanding of our nation's past.

GREAT HOUSES

The first residence in Chicago to qualify as a great house was the one built in 1836 (*below*) by Archibald Clybourne, the city constable and a pioneer in the meat-packing industry. Standing on what is now Elston Avenue, the twenty-room red brick mansion with its columned porch reflected the Virginia antecedents of its builder, and was indeed called "Old Virginia." The house was still intact in 1877 when it was described as "a veritable patriarch among its surroundings," but it disappeared not long afterward.

How quickly the concept of the great house took hold in Chicago is amply illustrated by this rare photograph of the Williams residence (*above*), which stood on the southeast corner of Monroe and Wabash. Constructed in 1843 for Eli B. Williams, a local official, this splendid example of Greek Revival architecture was the work of Edward Burling, who eventually went into partnership with Dankmar Adler, the colleague of Louis Sullivan. The Williams house survived for years as a fashionable restaurant called the Maison d'Orée, but was eventually swallowed up by the commercial expansion of the city.

In the 1850s, Chicagoans abandoned the Greek Revival and turned to the so-called Victorian style with its fancy iron work, bay windows, and cupolas. A good example of this new taste was Park Row (*below*) off Michigan Avenue near 12th Street. Among the city's most fashionable enclaves, Park Row survived the fire and later shared the location with the Illinois Central Station until, one by one, the old houses were demolished in the expansion of the station's parking lot.

Before the Great Fire, Michigan Avenue was essentially a residential quarter. In this view (*right*) looking north from Adams Street near the present Art Institute, it is possible to get a good idea of its old elegance. The house on the corner is that of Henry Hamilton Honoré, a Kentuckian who came to Chicago in 1855, made a fortune in real estate, and whose daughter Bertha became Mrs. Potter Palmer. It was from this house that she was married. In the distance projects the white marble mansion of William H. Browne, where President-elect and Mrs. Lincoln were entertained shortly before they left for Washington. All the houses on this block were destroyed in the fire. The People's Gas Building now occupies the site.

Rich and secure, Chicago continued to build throughout the Civil War. Typical of the mansions of this period was the one Leander McCormick constructed on Rush Street on the North Side in 1863. The brother of the great Cyrus of reaper fame, Leander was also active in the family business and is credited with conceiving the idea of putting a seat on the harvester. The family is shown here on their front steps, with Leander, the bearded man on the right. Their pose is significant, for in her memoir "Long Ago," published in Caroline Kirkland's anthology, *Chicago Yesterdays,* Mary Drummond recalled: "Another institution of our day was the custom of sitting on the front steps . . . for those of us who did not rejoice in porches and large grounds, they had their joys. . . ."

The front parlor of the McCormick residence (with Robert Hall McCormick, Leander's son, in the doorway) accurately reveals the taste of a fashionable Chicago family of the time. The curved white marble fireplace, the expanse of mirror, the flowered carpet, and the elaborately carved furniture were all considered *de rigueur*. The McCormick house perished in the Great Fire.

After the fire, many wealthy Chicagoans who had lived on Michigan Avenue and other downtown streets that were turned over to commerce, moved farther south. One of the places they went to was Aldine Square (*above*) on Vincennes Avenue between 38th and 39th Streets. It was the creation of the firm of Cudell and Blumenthal, headed by Adolph Cudell, a recent arrival from Aachen, Germany; its handsome uniform houses, facing a private park containing fine elms and an artificial lake, gave it a distinctly European feeling. No trace of either the houses or the bosky square now survives. They were replaced by low-cost housing in 1956.

The other choice South Side location was Prairie Avenue (*right*). Two miles from downtown, paralleling the tracks of the Illinois Central, it was, in a real sense, the Fifth Avenue of the whole Midwest. But not all of Prairie Avenue. The novelist Arthur Meeker, who grew up there, makes that very clear in *To Chicago with Love*: ". . . it would be well to define what we meant by early Prairie Avenue. On this point my mother was adamant. Although it was one of the longest arteries in the city, she always maintained that only the first six blocks from Sixteenth to Twenty-second Streets comprised 'The Sunny Street that held the Sifted Few.' " The house on the right belonged to Marshall Field and was designed by Richard Morris Hunt, architect to the Vanderbilts. When it was completed in 1876, the mansion cost $250,000 and later was the first residence in the city with electric lights. After serving as a center for the Bauhaus refugees from Hitler's Germany, it was demolished following the Second World War.

The Junoesqe lady attired as Cleopatra is Delia Spencer
Caton, the second Mrs. Marshall Field, a social leader
of Chicago's *Bal Masqué* years.

Undoubtedly the grandest house on Prairie Avenue was that of George M. Pullman, a Second Empire brownstone château which Arthur Meeker described in his novel *Prairie Avenue* as being reminiscent "of the Grand Opera in Paris." Originally constructed in 1873 by the Chicago contractor John M. Dunphy, the sleeping car magnate later had Solon S. Beman, the architect of the town of Pullman, add the large glass hothouse shown below and other dependencies. This 1912 photograph shows the ceremony marking the centennial of the Fort Dearborn massacre, taking place on the Pullman terrace. The massacre site was but yards away. George Pullman's palace was demolished in 1922 by his daughters.

This view of the entrance hall of the Pullman residence (*right*), taken from a family album, is a splendid example of the fine woodwork so dear to the hearts of nineteenth-century Chicagoans. It is a reflection of a time when a wave of German and Czech immigration had created an enormous reservoir of skilled cabinetmakers.

Above: The drawing room of the Pullman house, the white and gold saloon where the magnate delighted in giving receptions for several hundred people.

Below: The Red Room of the Pullman House, a typical upper-class Victorian combination of comfort and grandeur, of rockers and brocade, of family photographs and oil paintings.

Among the Prairie Avenue millionaires was John B. Sherman, "The Father of the Stock Yards." The house he commissioned in 1874 (*above*) was the first important work of two young architects who would help make Chicago building famous around the world, Daniel Burnham and John Wellborn Root. Its comparative simplicity, contrasting sharply with the Beaux Arts villas around it, drew the attention of another architect, Louis Sullivan. Its discovery is one of the key incidents in his *The Autobiography of an Idea:* ". . . in his eighteenth year . . . he had occasion one day to pass in the neighborhood of Prairie Avenue and Twenty-first Street. . . . There, on the southwest corner of the intersection, his eye was attracted by a residence, nearing completion, which seemed far better than the average run of such structures inasmuch as it exhibited a certain allure of style indicating personality." The Sherman residence disappeared in the twentieth-century looting of Prairie Avenue.

32

Those Chicagoans living north of the river before the fire generally rebuilt on their old property. The McCormicks had always been North Siders; indeed, at one time there were so many of the clan ensconced in the vicinity of Rush and Erie Streets that the neighborhood was familiarly referred to as "McCormickville." The focus of this gathering was the sumptuous brownstone dwelling (*left*) built for Cyrus Hall McCormick at 675 Rush Street, between 1875 and 1879. The architects were Cudell and Blumenthal, who took as their model one of the recently completed pavilions of the Louvre.

The dining room (*below*), like all the McCormick interiors, was the work of the fashionable New York decorating firm L. Marcott and Company. Cyrus McCormick lived only five years in his grand house, but his widow, Nettie Fowler McCormick, died there in 1923 at the age of eighty-eight. Afterward it was the home of her son, Harold F. McCormick, who had divorced Edith Rockefeller, the daughter of the first John D., and married the Polish opera singer Ganna Walska. Following the Second World War, the house was emptied of the treasures Harold McCormick had gathered—antique furniture, paintings, tapestries, a library of more than a million manuscript items relating to the McCormick family. In 1955 it was demolished.

The William Borden mansion at the corner of Lake Shore Drive and Bellevue Place (*left*) was Chicago's best example of a Richard Morris Hunt French Renaissance château. Built in 1884 for the lawyer and mining engineer who had made a fortune in Leadville, Colorado, it was also the home of his daughter Mary, the well-known novelist, and of his granddaughter Ellen, who married Adlai Stevenson. The gray limestone house was replaced by a nondescript apartment building in the early 1960s.

The Farwells, brothers and partners in the dry-goods and real estate business, built their houses (*below*) next to each other on Pearson Street, just north of the Water Tower. Charles B. Farwell's residence, on the left, was architecturally the more significant. The work of the Chicago firm of Treat and Foltz, it was a flamboyant, $100,000 example of the popular Queen Anne style, and when it was completed in 1882 was widely admired for its advanced steam-heating system, modern plumbing, and plate-glass windows. John V. Farwell's house on the right was destroyed for the widening of Michigan Avenue in the 1920s, but Charles's lingered into the '30s as a restaurant called Chez Louis. The entire site is now occupied by Bonwit Teller's store.

If one could magically reconstruct any of Chicago's lost great houses, the first choice would have to be the castle designed for the merchant, real estate tycoon, and hotel-man, Potter Palmer, and his brilliant consort. From the moment in 1882 when Henry Ives Cobb's crenelated edifice rose on Lake Shore Drive between Banks and Schiller Streets, it was the Windy City's Buckingham Palace. During the spacious summer of the 1893 Columbian Exposition, Bertha Honoré Palmer entertained here almost without pause. After her death in Florida in 1918, her casket was returned to the mansion under a blanket of orchids. In 1950, the wrecker's ball struck and the Palmer castle vanished into thin air.

The central hall of the Potter Palmer mansion, shown here (*left*) around 1900,
was Chicago's most magnificent residential interior. It was the perfect setting for
Mrs. Palmer, resplendent in diamond tiara and dog collar and her famous rope
of pearls, as she greeted visiting dignitaries such as President William McKinley or
artists such as Anders Zorn.

No room in the mansion was more famous than the 75-foot-long picture gallery
(*above*), Mrs. Palmer's special creation. It was her voice which Henry B. Fuller gave
to Susan Bates in his penetrating novel of Chicago society, *With the Procession*:
" 'Well, we might just stick our noses in the picture-gallery for a minute . . .
Some of these things are going to the Art Institute . . .' " With the help of her
friend the painter Mary Cassatt, Mrs. Palmer assembled the nucleus of the Art
Institute's rare French Impressionist collection, which will always, in a sense, be a
memorial to the chatelaine of this lost castle.

Among the architects who remained disciples of Louis Sullivan, one of the most interesting was George Maher. Arriving in Chicago in the 1870s, he was first associated with August Bauer, a one-time teacher of Dankmar Adler, and later was a colleague of Frank Lloyd Wright and George Grant Elmslie. The huge granite house Maher built in Evanston in 1901 (*right*) for James A. Patten, a patron of Northwestern University, was a product of his determination to produce an American style freed from European precedents. His advanced design was particularly evident in the startlingly modern looking stable (*right, below*). The imaginative use of the thistle motif in the glass and woodwork of the entrance hall (*below*), to suggest the Pattens' Scotch antecedents, was an outgrowth of Maher's interest in the Chicago arts and crafts movement. His astonishing Patten house was demolished in 1938.

39

Few architects have possessed a more perfect sense of scale than Chicago's master of the Beaux Arts tradition, David Adler. His first commission, in 1911, from an uncle, C. A. Stonehill, resulted in a delightful Louis XIII style château in Glencoe, north of the city (*right*). The pink-brick and white-stone residence, which stood on a high knoll overlooking Lake Michigan, was demolished in 1962.

Adler's Louis XVI style town house (*left*), built in 1921 on Astor Street for Joseph T. Ryerson, whose family helped to create Inland Steel, is a model of a city dwelling in the classical tradition. It would be difficult to name another American architect who could interpret a French salon more faultlessly than Adler did in the Ryerson drawing room (*below*). Though the Ryerson house is still standing, it has been divided into apartments, and the gracious ambiance of Astor Street, which included Louis Sullivan and Frank Lloyd Wright's Charnley house and John Wellborn Root's own residence, has been devastated by the intrusion of high-rise apartment buildings.

40

LITTLE HOUSES ON THE PRAIRIE

Left, above: A drawing of a typical dwelling in the French settlements of America's heartland. The first shelter Jean Baptiste Point Sable constructed on the site of Chicago in the eighteenth century most likely resembled this in some aspects, particularly in the vertical placement of the logs forming the walls.

Left, below: A rare pre-fire photograph of a balloon-frame house of Chicago's Greek Revival era. It stood at 19 East Monroe Street, now part of the Palmer House hotel block.

The charming house (*right*) and the four that follow were captured by an anonymous photographer in the early 1880s. The photographs reveal a fact too often forgotten: the vast majority of the newcomers who arrived in Chicago in the latter half of the nineteenth century from Europe and the older states of the East did not live in slums. Chicago was a town where a man who was willing to work could usually get a job, and the prairie west of the city was soon dotted with houses like these owned by working people. The dwelling at right, with its widow's walk recalling the coastal villages of Massachusetts, was most likely built by New Englanders. After the Civil War, when their small, stony farms could no longer compete with the products of the Midwest's rich soil, they arrived by the thousands from Massachusetts, New Hampshire, and Vermont.

44

Chicago's small houses impressed settlers and visitors because they were not built in
solid rows right on the street, but had a bit of space around them which permitted
them to be bathed in sunshine. The joyous loungers in the windows of the little
wooden house (*left, above*) and the dark-clad residents of the quaint brick cottage
(*left, below*) have a distinctly European air about them. The other two houses reveal,
by their ample size, the prosperity experienced by large numbers of Chicagoans
in the 1880s.

APARTMENTS

The Mecca (*left*), built on the South Side at State and 34th Streets in 1891, was the result of the collaboration of Frank Burnham and George Edbrooke, a leading warehouse and store designer. Its two soaring courts — a glory of glass and iron — were a brilliant solution to the problem of public space in a city with Chicago's harsh winters. When the Mecca was a sought-after address by Chicago's society, the courts were carpeted and boasted elaborate fountains; later, when this part of Chicago was occupied by blacks, the building gave its name to the "Mecca Flat Blues." The Mecca was destroyed in 1952 for the expansion of the Illinois Institute of Technology.

The Francis Apartments (*right, above*), also on the South Side, at 4304 South Forestville Avenue, were an important example of Frank Lloyd Wright's early work. Built in 1895, their superb iron grilles revealed the influence of Louis Sullivan's geometric designs. Though they had been designated a Chicago architectural landmark, the Francis Apartments were demolished in 1967.

This dining room (*right, below*) was in Mr. and Mrs. Samuel Marx's apartment on Astor Street. It was designed in 1938 by Mr. Marx, the architect responsible for interiors such as the legendary original Pump Room in the Ambassador East Hotel. The still life, part of the Marxes' important art collection, is by Matisse. The apartment has now been dismantled.

The **Galena and Chicago Railway Station,** the first in the city, was constructed in 1848 near Kinzie and Canal Streets. In the days before the telegraph, the line's president often posted himself in the cupola to spot incoming trains. The station survived as a railroad employees' reading room until the 1880s.

III

The Rails Reach Out

It is symbolic that Chicago's first railroad, the Galena and Chicago Union, was chartered a year before the city itself, for if there is any one factor responsible for Chicago's phenomenal growth it is the iron horse. That historic line put Galena first in its name, for Galena, an important river town, was then much larger than Chicago. This was, in fact, the beginning of the vast Chicago and North Western Railway, but it almost never got rolling. The year after the road was chartered a financial panic hit the country and it was the determination of one man, William Ogden, that saved it. But it took even a man with Ogden's vigor ten years to sell enough stock to make people realize that this was a serious undertaking, and it was not until September 1847 that the right of way was surveyed. It was Ogden who understood the importance of the railroad to the island that was Chicago, understood it as the Elizabethan sailors had understood the importance for England of the sea lanes to the Americas.

The way some men have a passion for women and others for food, Ogden had a passion for transportation. As mayor he had found unlimited worlds to conquer: Chicago's streets were undoubtedly among the worst in America. After a heavy rain or during the spring thaw, wagons and beasts and unwary citizens often sank a foot or more into the town's rich mud. It was not unusual to see signs proclaiming NO BOTTOM HERE or SHORTEST ROAD TO CHINA in even the busiest thoroughfares. Perhaps no story of early Chicago is more revealing than the one told about "Long John" Wentworth, the tall, witty New Hampshire-born editor, promoter, and politician who eventually became the city's mayor. One day a friend spotted "Long John" struggling in the all-engulfing muck and asked if he could help. "No, thanks," shouted back Wentworth, "I've a horse under me." As mayor, Ogden constructed more than a hundred miles of improved streets, threw dozens of bridges across the city's deep gutters, and backed the building of plank toll roads out into the country in every direction.

All of this was but prologue to the energies he put into the development of railroads, an interest which would one day make him president of the vast Union Pacific. When the first ten miles of Galena and Chicago track had been laid, Ogden brought to the city, lashed to the deck of a sailing vessel, a small locomotive with an enormous stack which he christened "The Pioneer." And pioneer it did, puffing along at the spine-tingling speed of twenty miles an hour while pulling a string of open wagons filled with local notables. After that demonstration, Chicagoans never again had to be convinced of the practicality of railroads. The Galena and Chicago was soon returning a handsome profit; by 1850 it had been extended to Elgin, some thirty miles away.

Now the lines spun out, like the strands of a stupendous iron web centered on the incipient metropolis at the foot of the lake: the Chicago and Rock Island; the Michigan Central; the Michigan Southern; the Pittsburgh, Fort Wayne and Chicago. None, though, could approach in importance the august Illinois Central. Construction of the new line began in December 1851 simultaneously at Chicago and Cairo, the city at the southern tip of the state where the Ohio flowed into the Mississippi. By 1856 Illinois Central trains were pulling into the heart of Chicago at Randolph Street, bringing with them the riches of the middle third of the continent and leaching business away from the city's chief rival, St. Louis. The names connected with the line read like a primer of American history. Daniel Webster, Stephen Douglas, and Henry Clay all had a hand in the legislation that led to its birth. George B. McClellan was its chief engineer, Abraham Lincoln a lawyer on its staff, Mark Twain a pilot on one of its steam packets. And it was an Illinois Central train, the "Cannon Ball," which Casey Jones drove that fateful April morning in 1900.

By the middle '50s nearly 3000 miles of track touched Chicago, and 96 trains a day came and went over its ten trunk and eleven branch lines. In these years more miles of railroad were constructed in Illinois than in any other state in the Union, and soon ten thousand miles of track connected Chicago with all the important commercial centers in the country. The Mississippi was bound to it at sixteen points; by the time of the Civil War, the city had 820 locomotives and 1500 cars in its yards, and passenger fares alone were annually bringing in $65 million.

In combination with Samuel F. B. Morse's new telegraph, the nerve center of Chicago could dispatch boxcars to carry corn and wheat and cattle and hogs and oats as they were needed, boxcars to carry McCormick's reapers, boxcars to carry shoes and glass and furniture. Chicago became the bowknot at the center of the country, from which the wealth-bringing ribbons of iron stretched east to the Atlantic, south to the Gulf, north to Canada, and eventually west to the Pacific. Ogden's dream had become a reality. Snow and mud were no longer problems; months were added each year to the commercial activity of the city. The journal *The Prairie Farmer* did not let the achievement go unsung:

> *Our horses now freed from the road-dragging toil,*
> *We will keep on the fallows, and till well the soil,*
> *And when we have leisure the city to greet,*
> *With our ladies we'll then in the cars take a seat.*

> *Now free from the dread of the mud and the*
>   *slough,*
> *Feeling sure that the rail-car will carry us through;*
> *Then welcome the steam horse with sinews so*
>   *strong,*
> *Ourselves and our produce can now move along.*

No American city was linked to the romance of the railroad the way Chicago was. It resembled the imperial European centers — Paris, for instance — where the stations, like the points of a gigantic compass, beckoned in all directions: Gare de l'Est, Gare du Nord, Gare de Lyon. In Chicago it was the Dearborn, the La Salle, the North Western. Here, in time, like the ocean liners of New York slipping their Hudson River berths, the superb trains would head out to Boston and Montreal, to Los Angeles and Seattle, those majestic trains — the Broadway Limited, the Twentieth Century, the Panama Limited, the Chief and the Super Chief, the Overland, the Aristocrat, the Royal Palm, the Denver Zephyr, the City of New Orleans. None carried the name of Chicago, for it was not their destination. Chicago was where they all began.

It was the railroad that made Chicago the capital of America's heartland, its attainable metropolis, its possible dream. The United States has had a handful of such cities — Boston for New England, San Fran-

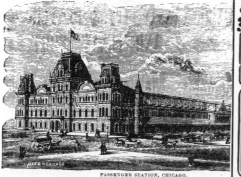

cisco for the West Coast, New Orleans for the Gulf. They are the nation's most interesting cities, these provincial capitals. It was not of New York that the inhabitants of Peoria and Mattoon and Kokomo and Goshen and Cedar Rapids and Blooming Prairie thought when the cars went by at night, lit up, affording tantalizing glimpses of flashing silver and cut flowers and sparkling glasses of ice water. For nearly a century the trains would be a brilliant advertisement for Chicago, would draw to it like a moving magnet the young men and women of the farms and hamlets for a thousand miles around where the land was drained by the Wabash, the Skunk, the Maumee, and the Sangamon.

The railroads did something else too; they helped to change the way Chicago looked. The 1850s had witnessed the full flowering of the Greek Revival city, but the Greek Revival had its limitations. In the surviving pre-fire photographs, the style is shown working perfectly for the little State Street shops selling hoopskirts and washbasins and for real estate and lawyers' offices. But, for all intents and purposes, these are the shops of a village, serving an area as limited in its way as the small Greek city-states which first bred the style. Chicago was no longer a city-state but the capital of an empire. The railroads made it possible for a company's central office to serve the needs of thousands of scattered villages. This demanded structures that could house the hundreds of white-collar workers who helped swell Chicago's population from 28,000 in 1850 to 100,000 ten years later. The Greek Revival did not readily expand to office building size.

This sudden change in the requirements of American business coincided with a revolutionary shift in taste. The reign of the Greek Revival had not been unchallenged. Americans had long been fascinated by the pseudo-Gothic structures which had begun to be built in England in the middle of the eighteenth century. In 1838, the American architect Alexander Jackson Davis had constructed a castlelike extravaganza, Lyndhurst, on the Hudson above New York City; in 1846, Richard Upjohn had made a dramatic Gothic statement with his Trinity Church at the head of Wall Street. If one could think of the Parthenon and Chartres at the same time, it was no great step to include also Egypt's Temple of Karnak, the Roman Forum, the palaces of Venice, or anything else that might strike one's fancy. And that is just what was

happening in the world of fashion at this time. Now, instead of manuals on the Greek style alone, the builder could take his choice from a veritable department store of tastes. There were Andrew Jackson Downing's *Cottage Residences,* plumping for the Gothic; John Ruskin's *The Stones of Venice;* Viollet-le-Duc's *Dictionary of French Architecture from the Eleventh to the Sixteenth Centuries;* and Calvert Vaux's *Villas and Cottages* coming down on the side of the Italianate. For the architects of the period, it was a rich, tempting, and very dangerous mélange.

There was one more element in this astonishing change of scene and that was the rapid technological development of the period which readily permitted the construction of buildings of five and six and seven stories, allowed glass to be made in ever-larger sheets, and facilitated the carving of wood in a fantasticality of shapes. None, though, had a more profound effect than the complete cast-iron fronts that began arriving from New York in the 1850s. Painted white in imitation of marble, these precast *palazzi* came in any style the builder wanted: Classical, Italianate, or Gothic. They were turned out mile upon mile, with arches and columns and brackets and acanthus leaves enough to satisfy even the greediest client. Chicago, the city that had given the world the balloon frame, readily accepted all of these innovations and all these styles. They were evident in the new office buildings springing up close to one another on State, Dearborn, Clark, and La Salle Streets. There they stood — Cobb's, Dickey's, Link's, Garrett's, Magies', the Honoré — splendid from their high, cast-iron first floors past their five ranks of crowded windows with ornamental lintels, up to their heavy bracketed cornices and flat galvanized iron roofs.

Nowhere, though, was the new taste — which has been termed variously Reign of Terror, Gingerbread, Victorian, and Parvenu — more evident than in domestic architecture. All the restrained features of the Greek Revival were quickly abandoned. The square or oblong shape of the house persisted for a time, but the classic cornice and the returns were lost almost at once. In their place came a heavy, overhanging cornice with scroll-sawn brackets. Next, corner pilasters disappeared and the verandahs, which replaced the columned porches, became ever more elaborate. Ceilings, as though expressing new wealth, rose higher and higher, while windows, their tops now arched, grew taller and thinner. Capping it all was a forest of elaborate chimneys, a mansard roof instead of the simple low gables of the past and, if the owner was rich enough, a cupola. This was the ideal of the villas rising in the new suburbs of Hyde Park and Kenwood, of Lake View and Evanston. It could be seen on fashionable Park Row just off Michigan Avenue and in the grand quarters of the North Side.

Even the pride of the city, the Court House, did not escape this revolution in taste. When Van Osdel had built it in the early 1850s, it was a fine, direct Greek Revival structure, but just before the great fire he added two vast wings and an enormous cupola and labeled the whole thing "French." If Van Osdel could follow fashion, so too could his greatest con-temporary, Edward Burling, the architect who had built that jewel of the Greek Revival city, the splendid Eli B. Williams house. Now, at the southeast corner of Washington and La Salle Streets, he designed in the French style a handsome building to house the Chamber of Commerce and the Board of Trade. Three stories high, it was constructed of the favorite material of the new city — limestone from the Lemont quarries in Cook County, called by its promoters "Athens marble." Burling's unfailing good taste is important in the history of Chicago, for into Burling's office would come Dankmar Adler and into Dankmar Adler's office would come Louis Sullivan and into Louis Sullivan's office would come Frank Lloyd Wright.

The Age of the Iron Horse

"That's my Middle West — not the wheat or the prairies or the lost Swede towns, but the thrilling returning trains of my youth," says the narrator of F. Scott Fitzgerald's *The Great Gatsby,* and then goes on to recall his Christmas passages through Chicago's "old dim Union Station." The Union was Fitzgerald's own transfer point on his way home to St. Paul, Minnesota, from Princeton, New Jersey. Chicago was a city permeated by the romance of the rails. Even a partial listing of the lines which served it rings like an American geography lesson: Pennsylvania; Baltimore & Ohio; Gulf, Mobile; Chicago, Burlington & Quincy; Norfolk & Western; Erie, Lackawanna: New York Central; The Soo; Atchison, Topeka & **Santa** Fe; Illinois Central.

Below: Trains ready for departure at the Illinois Central's Randolph Street Depot about 1890.

THE STATIONS

Above: The Chicago & North Western Station at Wells and Kinzie Streets shortly after completion in 1881. The home of the crack San Francisco Overland and the Portland Rose, it was abandoned in 1911 and the Merchandise Mart now occupies the site.

Below: The Lake Shore & Michigan Southern & Rock Island Depot, erected in 1873 at Van Buren and Sherman Streets. The Rock Island had made history in 1856 by constructing the first bridge across the Mississippi. The old depot was superseded in 1903 by the La Salle Street Station.

Theodore Dreiser, in *A Book About Myself,* recalled:
". . . we would make our way to the great railway station
at the end of Dearborn Street, where a tall clock-tower held
a single yellow clock-face." The most picturesque of Chicago
stations, the Dearborn (*left*) was designed in 1882 by Cyrus
L. W. Eidlitz, the architect of the *New York Times* building
on Times Square, to serve among other lines the Atchison,
Topeka & Santa Fe. The brave tower is now truncated and
the station's peaked roofs have disappeared.

The gateway to the city from the south was the Illinois
Central Depot (*below*), built in 1892 by Bradford L. Gilbert
of New York. The familiar landmark at Michigan Avenue
and 12th Street was razed in 1974.

Architecturally, no other Chicago station approached Solon S. Beman's monumental Grand Central of 1890. Its Norman tower, rising 247 feet at the corner of Harrison and Wells Streets, contained an 11,000-pound bell to warn travelers of the time, and its iron-and-glass train shed was one of the marvels of nineteenth-century engineering. The station also housed a deluxe hotel and was the departure point for the Baltimore & Ohio's all-Pullman Capital Limited, the favored transport of Washington-bound Midwest politicians. The prominent Chicago architect Harry Weese called the razing of Grand Central in 1971 an act of "wanton destruction."

THE TRAINS

The Santa Fe's sleek Super Chief (*below*) at the Dearborn Station in the late 1940s, ready for its thirty-nine-and-a-half-hour run to Los Angeles.

Above: The Panama Limited, leaving the Illinois Central Station in 1916 with a load of passengers determined to enjoy themselves in the sunny south.

Below: The most glamorous of American trains, the Twentieth Century Limited, leaving the La Salle Street Station in 1939. This Chicago–to–New York streamliner was given a kind of immortality by a Ben Hecht–Charles MacArthur movie.

The Twentieth Century achieved a rare sophistication when it was redesigned by
Henry Dreyfus in 1938. *Above:* The Dreyfus-designed observation car. Like so many
of the magnificent trains, the Twentieth Century Limited rolled into oblivion in
the 1960s.

THE KINGDOM OF PULLMAN

In 1880, on 4300 acres just south of Chicago, George
Pullman began building a model industrial town. By the
time he was finished, Pullman contained not only workers'
housing and a vast sleeping-car plant, but a library, hotel,
theatre, school, hospital, market, and a church. The administration building (*right*), like all the structures in the town,
was designed by Solon S. Beman. It faced man-made three-
acre Lake Vista, from whose center a tall column of water
shot into the air, propelled by the great Corliss Engine that
Pullman had brought back from the Philadelphia Centennial Exposition of 1876. The administration building still
stands, but Beman's unusual water tower, which looms in
the background, has been demolished, and Lake Vista and
its curved drive disappeared with the extension of Cottage
Grove Avenue.

The Santa Barbara (*opposite*), built by Pullman for the Southern Pacific in 1887, gloried in seats upholstered in red mohair and cabinet work of mahogany, oak, and satinwood. Light was provided by kerosene lamps and heat by coal stoves.

Typical of the private cars of the Gilded Age was the one (*below*) the firm fashioned for Porfirio Díaz, the Mexican dictator, in 1897.

Pullman was as famous for its dining cars as for its sleepers. This photograph (*below*), taken in the 1920s, has all of the company's well-known hallmarks: the spotless napery, the heavy silver, the white-coated black waiter.

"Whenever the traffic of the city growing so magically upon its banks had burst its bounds, the river was spanned by a red-wooden turn-bridge . . . To stand on the Rush Street Bridge at nightfall was . . . a joy indeed to the lover of ships." — Hobart Chatfield-Taylor, *Chicago*. The city remained a major port throughout the nineteenth century, its waterways — the Great Lakes to the north and east and the Mississippi system to the south and west — making it a kind of American Suez. This view, looking east from the Rush Street Bridge around 1869, makes it clear why first-time visitors were startled to see, in the heart of the continent, a scene reminiscent of the wharves of New York and Boston.

IV
Queen of the Lakes

CHICAGO had need of all these new offices and houses and public buildings, for now still more infusions swelled its population. On a single summer day in 1857, 3400 foreign immigrants arrived on the Michigan Central Railroad. To the French and the Yankees were added Scandinavians and Belgians and Slavs; English and Irish poured in on the Black Ball packets from Liverpool, and Germans on the ships operated by the Chicago bankers Henry and Elias Greenebaum out of Bremen and Hamburg. Soon Chicago, with only 46 percent of its population native born, was more cosmopolitan than New York.

The Irish were the first of the new wave to settle in large numbers; driven by hunger and British oppression, they came by the hundreds from Waterford and Cork and Limerick. For the most part unskilled, they crowded into the Bridgeport area called "Back-of-the-Yards," where their political allegiance caused them to be termed "unwashed Dimmycrats." The Irish became the soldiers of the Democratic party organi-

zation and would supply the city with the stuff of its political legends: "Bathhouse John" Coughlin, "Hinky Dink" Kenna, Pat Nash, Ed Kelly, Martin Kennelly, and Richard J. Daley. In a city where the first church had been Roman Catholic and where men were generally judged by what they could do rather than who their fathers were, the Irish found advancement easier than in the eastern states. The NO IRISH NEED APPLY sign, with which the Boston Brahmins attempted to protect their social and economic hegemony, was unknown in Chicago.

The Irish Catholics were not the only oppressed group who found Chicago a haven. The city's first Jews had arrived in 1841, and six years later a synagogue, Kehilath Anshe Mayriv, the Congregation of the Men of the West, was established. Anti-Semitism seems to have been rare in the city. Abraham Kohn was clerk of the Common Council in the 1860s, and men such as the packer Nelson Morris, department store executive Leon Mandel, the Florsheims of shoe fame, the Regensteins of the window envelope, Moses Bensinger of the Brunswick sporting goods company, Philip Block of Inland Steel, Governor Henry Horner, and Julius Rosenwald of Sears, Roebuck would play an important part in the city's life.

The great majority of the Jews who came to Chicago in these years were from Germany, and it was the Germans of all faiths who, of the newly arrived groups, made the most profound impact on the city. There were Germans in Chicago as early as the 1830s, but it was the combination of the failure of the liberal revolutions of 1848 and disastrous economic conditions in the Rhineland that drove them to America in great numbers. By the late 1840s the Common Council found it necessary to have German-speaking tax collectors in some sections of the city and most large shops soon had at least one German-speaking clerk. In 1850, more than 17 percent of the population was German-born, and the foundations of a German city within the city had been laid. Generally literate and skilled, the Germans quickly established their own cultural institutions: churches, schools, hospitals, theatres, and, above all, musical organizations such as those that made the Saengerfests in Wright's Grove nationally famous. In 1851, the *Illinois Staats-Zeitung,* one of the most illustrious foreign language newspapers in the United States, began publication. It was the Germans, too, in the trade union movement and later in the Socialist party, who made many of the most eloquent appeals for economic justice in Chicago.

The Germans also had an indelible impact on the city's architecture. There can be no doubt that this vast Rhinelander migration contributed a great deal to the love of rough stone walls, heavy arches, and towers which became a hallmark of Chicago and other midwestern centers. The city was soon rich with German-born architects: Edward Baumann, Cord Gottig, August Bauer, and Otto Matz, who, as the first official architect for the Illinois Central Railroad designed its terminal at the foot of South Water Street.

The meeting places of the city's disparate elements, of recent immigrants and cattle kings, of wheat speculators and lumbermen, were the new mammoth hotels. Nothing more clearly symbolizes the booming metropolis of the late '50s and '60s. The Chicago hotel was, almost without exception, built to serve the railways. To find its equivalent, it is necessary to look abroad to the great caravansaries such as London's Charing Cross and the Grosvenor at Victoria Station. The note of grandeur had first been set by the second Tremont House, but it soon had keen competition from a dozen other equally opulent hostelries. There was the Briggs House, a vaguely Gothic structure on the northeast corner of Randolph and Wells, whose dining room offered such delights as roast prairie chicken and Glace Jenny Lind. There were the handsome Clarendon, the proper Adams House, the St. James, the Burlington, and the sumptuous Richmond House at the corner of South Water Street and Michigan Avenue where, in 1860, Albert Edward, Prince of Wales, stayed. Queen Victoria's nineteen-year-old-son became tongue-tied when he stepped out onto one of the hotel's balconies to face an assembled throng of enthusiastic Chicagoans, but blunt old John Wentworth had a remedy for that. "Say something to 'em, sonny," the Mayor ordered, slapping the heir to the British throne on the back.

Horace Greeley, the hopelessly peripatetic editor of the New York *Tribune,* had won the city's heart in 1858 by declaring that Chicago could boast at least half a dozen hotels that were better than anything New York could claim prior to the opening of the Astor. And that was before the two masterworks of the supreme architect of the Chicago hotel, William Boyington, had been built. The first of these, the huge Sherman House at the corner of Clark and Randolph, rose up in six stories of finely cut Athens marble, could accommodate 300 guests, and always had an orchestra playing in its grand dining room. But Boyington's chef-d'oeuvre was the opulent Grand Pacific, whose roof was put on just before the great fire. Turning for inspiration to the extensions of the Louvre just completed for Napoleon III by Louis Visconti and Hector Martin Lefuel, Boyington created an edifice which would be a model for Chicago hotels for years to come. In a daring display of prodigality, he brought together Doric, Ionic, and Corinthian columns, balconies, domes, pavilions, a forest of chimneys, and caryatids to compose a building which had, in the words of a contemporary guide to the city, not one, but "four grand entrances." Here was indeed a palace for the people.

It was no easy task to reach these magnificent hostelries, for if the city's head and shoulders were of Athens marble, its feet were still of mud. Though Mayor Ogden had tried valiantly to improve the quagmire streets, Chicago's swampy, water-logged soil defied all solutions. Finally, in desperation, the City Council in 1856 ordered all grades to be raised to a height that would insure proper drainage. This was a costly proposition, for it was quickly estimated that the ordinance would force the lifting of street levels from four to seven feet. But there was no alternative. With the use of mud dredged from the bed of the Chicago River, the streets rose like the levees along the lower Mississippi. The Court House square was the first to be raised, leaving the buildings surrounding it set in sunken gardens, with their second stories now at street level. Once more Chicago's ingenuity was called on. Vacant lots were quickly filled in and houses built at the new level; ground floors were buried, turned into instant basements, and new floors added on top of the old. This worked well enough for residences, but it scarcely filled the bill when it came to five- and six-story office buildings and hotels.

The new challenge coincided with the arrival of another of those men whom destiny brought to Chicago at the right time. It had been that way with the organization of the packing industry, with the reaper, and now it was George Pullman's turn. The son of a Brockton, New York, mechanic, Pullman had been a cabinetmaker and house mover. He arrived in Chicago just as the ordinance raising the grade went into effect, and he found a city in which the owners of large downtown buildings were frantic from fear of losing their grand first floors with their high rents to the new level. None were more disturbed than the proprietors of the palatial Tremont House. Pullman walked around the building and then went inside and asked for the manager. "I can raise your hotel without breaking a single pane of window glass or stopping your business for a day," he told the astonished man. The owners of the Tremont were skeptical, but they were also desperate, and they had little choice but to give this brash, young newcomer a chance. Placing twelve hundred men with large jackscrews around the perimeter of the hotel, Pullman ordered each one to move his screw half-a-turn, a fraction of an inch, on his command. Slowly, almost imperceptibly, the five-story brick building rose into the air until it was at the level of the new grade; then a new foundation was placed under it. The attendant publicity created Pullman's first fortune, and he was soon levitating entire blocks. The nation watched in astonishment as Chicago miraculously pulled itself out of the primordial muck.

But destiny had not brought George Pullman to Chicago to be merely a lifter of buildings. His twin trades of cabinetmaking and house moving had sparked an idea more wondrous than that. Pullman knew that Chicago was the port from which the trains sailed out in all directions. He knew, also, that it was the city that set the standards for hotel comfort and luxury. Pullman wanted to wed those two things; to put the Sherman and the Tremont and the Richmond on wheels and send them out across the prairie. In 1859 he asked the Chicago and Alton Railroad for permission to make over some of its day coaches into sleeping cars with rows of upper and lower berths. The line replied that the idea was expensive nonsense: no passenger would pay extra to sleep on a train. But Pullman did not give up. Taking over an abandoned repair shop, he called into play his skill as a cabinetmaker to create the most beautiful railway car in the world. Of splendidly carved black walnut, its ceiling handsomely frescoed, its floors carpeted, Pullman's "Palace Car" boasted two drawing rooms, the most modern lavatories, and sumptuously upholstered seats which converted into beds. He spent $18,000 of his own money on the car, and, like Ogden with his first locomotive, he christened it "The Pioneer." The press hailed The Pioneer as a marvel, but again the railroad men said that it was too expensive, as well as too high for their bridges and too wide for their station platforms. Like a sorcerer who had conjured up something out of its time, George Pullman carefully put away his splendid creation. It would wait, gleaming and glorious, until 1865, when an awesome occasion would call it forth.

If Chicago was not ready for Pullman's sleeping car, it was unstinting in praise of what his jackscrews had done for the city. With the major buildings lifted a full story into the air and set upon new foundations, the downtown streets were now high and dry. The change was noted with pleasure by the thousands of prosperous farmers and small-town merchants, lawyers, doctors, and bankers who now looked to Chicago to break the monotony of life in Dubuque, Racine, and Muncie. Typical of them was a tall, thin young attorney from Springfield. Whenever Abraham Lincoln got up to Chicago on business — usually a case for the Illinois Central — he almost always found time for a show.

Undoubtedly, the grandest theatre in Chicago at this time was McVicker's. A handsome $85,000 brick structure on Madison Street, just west of State, McVicker's exterior boasted twin cupolas, while its interior was brightened by a drop curtain depicting the railroad bridge connecting Rock Island, Illinois, and Davenport, Iowa. The house featured a stock company headed by James H. McVicker himself, and was soon attracting stars of the magnitude of E. A. Sothern and Lotta Crabtree; in 1858, Edwin Booth headed the bill in *Brutus* and *Richelieu*. Ultimately, he would play Romeo to McVicker's daughter Mary's Juliet, and, as though to prove that life follows art, would marry her.

If Chicago was the entertainment capital of the heartland, it was, almost from the beginning, also the shopping center. As early as 1840, ladies wishing something smart to wear could find at Gray and Company cambrics, merinos, and satinets, not to mention Vauxhall Cloaks and palm leaf hats. If their palates also craved luxuries, Lefort's "Parisian Establishment" offered a wide selection of chocolates, sultanas, and nougats, as well as a confection called a "pyramid." In the midst of the 1847 building boom, the infant city had, along with $88,000 worth of iron and nails, brought in $68,000 worth of hats, capes, and furs and $51,000 worth of jewelry.

Yet, as the old Sauganash gave way to the Briggs House and the city's first primitive theatres were eclipsed by the splendor of McVicker's, so the little shops of the '40s were about to be overshadowed by the behemoth of the department store. One man, Potter Palmer, was chiefly responsible for the transition. Born of Quaker parents in New York state, Palmer learned his trade from the highly successful New York City merchant A. T. Stewart, and when he came to Chicago in 1852 with $5000, he was prepared to revolutionize the selling of dry goods. Palmer was Chicago's first shopkeeper to appeal primarily to women. His store on Lake Street was the first to have tastefully decorated show windows, to sell goods on credit, and to guarantee that if a customer was dissatisfied with merchandise it could be exchanged or her money refunded.

As time passed, Palmer's interest shifted more and more to real estate development, centering on his dream of making State Street Chicago's supreme shopping avenue. To help him run his department store, he brought in two young men as partners, Marshall

Field and Levi Leiter. Before long Potter Palmer had retired altogether from the retail business, and in 1863 he built for Field and Leiter — on State Street naturally — an elegant white marble palace which he rented to them for the then unheard-of sum of $50,000 a year. Here was the beginning of Marshall Field and Company.

This booming, bustling town was strongly Democratic, having been born during the heady days of Andrew Jackson's administration and agreeing with him wholeheartedly in his dislike and distrust of the so-called eastern aristocracy. The city found its spokesman in Stephen A. Douglas, the five-foot-tall senator from Illinois. It was Douglas who, as the powerful chairman of the Committee of Territories, pushed through statehood for territory after territory to place Chicago in the center of an "ocean-bound republic"; it was Douglas who fought for the city as the eastern terminus of the great transcontinental rail lines, fought for it against Memphis, New Orleans, and St. Louis. Yet it would be a single issue, the supreme issue, that would destroy him — slavery.

The growing controversy over slavery could not fail to erode the once almost unanimous support the Democrats had enjoyed in Chicago. The institution was profoundly hated in the city: by the Germans because many were liberals who had escaped from Prussian oppression, by the growing number of Scandinavians — Norwegians, Danes, Swedes — who had come to Chicago carrying a deep loathing of their native aristocracy, by the Yankees who were often dedicated abolitionists. In 1856, while Illinois was backing the Democrat James Buchanan for President, Chicago turned to the Free Soil advocate, John C. Frémont. That summer Abraham Lincoln had been in Chicago. He had come to speak at a banquet for Frémont — to speak against slavery:

The human heart is with us; God is with us. We shall again be able not to declare that "all states as states are equal," nor yet that "all citizens as citizens are equal," but to renew the broader, better declaration . . . that "all men are created equal."

If the diminutive Stephen Douglas was, as his admirers called him, the "Little Giant," then perhaps the new Republican party had found a giant killer.

The first great confrontation came in the senatorial election of 1858. In April of that year, the Democrats nominated Douglas for another term, and in June the Republicans named Lincoln. A month later, Douglas returned to Chicago from Washington and was given a hero's welcome by a throng from Little Egypt, as downstate Illinois was called because of its metropolis, Cairo. Up Lake Street the crowd moved with its idol to Wabash, Washington, down Dearborn to the Tremont House. Stepping out onto a balcony, Douglas eloquently defended his concept of "popular sovereignty," arguing that each state, individually, should decide whether it wanted to be slave or free.

Standing silently in the crowd, listening, was Lincoln. The next night he stepped out onto the same balcony. His words were very different from those of the "Little Giant": he spoke of the Union, of one law for all; he warned that "a house divided against itself cannot stand." The crowd that night was overwhelmingly Chicagoan, and now it was its turn to shout for its candidate, for "Honest Abe," as the people had begun to call him. Thus the great Lincoln-Douglas debates began. Chicago once more voted Republican, but Illinois went Democratic and Douglas was returned to the United States Senate. But it was only a battle that was lost, not a war.

Lincoln and Douglas would face each other again in 1860 as the presidential standard bearers of their two parties. It was as though Chicago, which a mere thirty years before had been a blowing field of wild onions, now bestrode the nation. The Democrats met in Baltimore, but it was Chicago for the Republicans, the first national political convention held in the city that would become America's number one convention town, the site of the selection of Grant, Garfield, Cleveland, Benjamin Harrison, Theodore Roosevelt, Taft, Harding, Franklin Delano Roosevelt, Eisenhower, as well as those vice presidents who moved up to the highest office in the land, Arthur, Coolidge, and Truman.

Chicago sought the convention because it was a Republican city, but also because it wanted to show off. With its population quadrupled to more than 100,000, with its fifteen railroads bringing in the wealth of Kansas, Missouri, Iowa, Minnesota, Wisconsin, and Nebraska, with its wholesale houses sending their own drummers into St. Louis and Cincinnati, underbidding local manufacturers and bringing back orders that kept 500 factories booming day and night, Chicago was in no mood to be different. The island had done all right. It was proud when men such as

William Howard Russell of the august London *Times* came out for a visit in 1860 and took seriously the title it had bestowed upon itself:

The scene now began to change gradually as we approached Chicago, the prairie subsided into swampy land, and thick belts of trees fringed the horizon; on our right glimpses of the sea could be caught through openings in the wood — the inland sea on which stands the Queen of the Lakes.

The "Queen of the Lakes" wanted to take her visitors to the Sherman House to mingle with Cyrus McCormick, William Ogden, and Nelson Morris — men who could match dollars with almost anyone New York or Boston could present. Besides, the dining room featured fresh lobster, chilled champagne, and pheasant under glass. She wanted the visitors to see Elijah Peacock's dazzling jewelry store on Randolph Street with its trays of Brazilian diamonds and pigeon-blood rubies. She wanted to suggest an evening at McVicker's, where one night Adah Isaacs Menken was performing in *Mazeppa's Ride* and, on the next, the extraordinary New Orleans pianist Louis Moreau Gottschalk was charming the city with his syncopated compositions. The more serious minded might drive down to Cottage Grove Avenue and Thirty-fourth Street to see the astonishing Gothic castle William Boyington had just built for the new University of Chicago.

The city had every right to be pleased with itself that May day in 1860 when the Republican National Convention convened in the Wigwam, a plain pine structure which the local Republican Club had built on the site of Mark Beaubien's Sauganash Hotel. The ladies of Chicago had attempted to disguise the hall's utilitarian lines by covering as much of it as possible with garlands, wreaths, flags, marble busts, and portraits of American notables. And just to add a touch of history, the official gavel was fashioned from a timber of the *Niagara*, Commodore Perry's flagship in the Battle of Lake Erie.

It is unlikely that any of the ten thousand Republicans who crowded into the Wigwam were very much concerned with aesthetics. For days the city had been a maelstrom of political parades, processions for New York's favorite son, William H. Seward; for the popular Ohio governor, Salmon P. Chase; for John C. Frémont; for Illinois's own Abraham Lincoln. And there was no dearth of marchers. More than 2000 people came out from New York alone. Every one of Chicago's railroads offered special excursion rates for those who wanted to see the convention and the city. The trains from New England stretched for miles around the south end of the lake into Indiana. This was, in a sense, Chicago's first great fair. The new city, as well as the new party, had attracted the whole country. Chicago, as a single man, wanted Lincoln, the Illinois candidate, the rail-splitter. It took three ballots, but on the third he won. In a moment of wild enthusiasm, a man climbed up through a skylight in the Wigwam's roof and passed the triumphant word to the crowd packed in the streets below. When he was told, Lincoln took it calmly. "Just think," he said, "of such a sucker as me as President."

In the election, Chicago gave Lincoln ten thousand votes to two thousand for its old hero Douglas. And when Fort Sumter was fired on, Joseph Medill's *Tribune*, which had been one of the first newspapers to support Lincoln, set the tone:

Let expressed rebuke and contempt rest on every man weak enough to be anywhere else in this crisis than on the side of the country against treason . . . We say to the tories and the lickspittles in this community, a patient and reluctant, but at last an outraged and maddened people will no longer endure your hissing. You must keep your venom sealed, or go down! *The gates of Janus are open, the storm is on us. Let the cry be:* THE SWORD OF THE LORD AND OF GIDEON!

The gates of Janus were indeed opened, and the sword of the Lord — his fiery, swift sword — was quickly unsheathed. When Lincoln called for volunteers, Governor Richard Yates found that Chicago alone was ready to supply the entire six regiments he had requested. Sumter surrendered on the thirteenth of April and a week later the first Chicagoans, numbering some 600, boarded an Illinois Central train and headed south. Eventually, Chicago sent some 22,000 troops to fight for Lincoln, to fight at Fort Donelson and Chickamauga, at Shiloh and Vicksburg, at Pea Ridge and Malvern Hill. More than 3000 did not return.

Yet the Civil War was, without doubt, a great economic boon for the city; the bloody conflict between the nation's two halves was the event which finally raised Chicago to dominance in the heartland. While its rivals — Louisville, Cincinnati, and St. Louis — were all border cities whose river trade was disrupted by the war, Chicago, far to the north, with its untrammeled railroads, flourished. The city became the chief supplier of the Union army, and eastern investors, spotting a good thing, poured money into its plants and warehouses.

Throughout the bloodshed, Chicago never stopped building. The huge Union Stock Yards at Halsted and Thirty-ninth streets was constructed. There were new additions to the university, a vast hall for the 1864 Democratic convention, Uranus Crosby's magnificent $600,000 opera house, the refurbishing of hotels such as the Tremont, and the erection of splendid mansions like the one Leander, Cyrus McCormick's brother, built on Rush Street. And daily, factories, warehouses, and grain elevators grew ever thicker along the river.

As victory seemed nearer and nearer, as Atlanta and then Richmond fell, Chicago waited expectantly. When news of Appomattox came, the crowds in the streets sang first the Doxology and then "The Battle-Cry of Freedom," composed in the dark summer of 1862 by the city's own George F. Root in his office at Root and Cady, music publishers, on Clark Street:

> *Yes, we'll rally 'round the flag boys,*
> *We'll rally once again,*
> *Shouting the Battle-cry of Freedom!*

Then at the moment of triumph, when it seemed true indeed that the Union dead had not died in vain, one last life was added to their awesome number.

Chicago got word of Lincoln's assassination early in the morning of April 16. Like a whirling carousel whose works have jammed, all motion ceased. The saloons, the theatres, shops, the Board of Trade, the courts, all closed. The city waited as the funeral train slowly wound its way westward — Baltimore, Harrisburg, Philadelphia, New York, Albany, Buffalo, Cleveland, Columbus, Indianapolis — and then, on the morning of May 1, over the tracks of his own Illinois Central, the black-palled cars reached Chicago and stopped at Park Row, just off Michigan Avenue. The afternoon before he was shot, Lincoln had gone for a drive with his wife Mary and told her: "with God's blessing we may hope for four years of peace and happiness, then we will go back to Illinois, and pass the rest of our lives in quiet." Now he was back, for that spring, for that summer, for the ages.

Witnesses reported that the city was eerily quiet, a quiet like that stillness which descended at Appomattox when, at last, the guns fell silent. It had been raining, the heavy spring rain of Illinois which is guaranteed to make the corn "knee high by the Fourth of July," and the streets once again were muddy. Yet few rode that day. The citizens of Chicago walked like kings come to bury a fellow monarch. There were young women in white dresses before the black-plumed hearse; there were soldiers just returned from battle; there were distinguished pallbearers, his old friends such as Mayor John Wentworth and Francis Sherman, at whose hotel he had often dined, and John B. Rice, who presented the plays he so enjoyed. In all, forty thousand walked with him to Van Osdel's Court House, and there a quarter of a million moved silently past the ebony and silver coffin to glimpse his chalk-white face. Yet there was one sound, a sound that all who heard it never forgot; it was, in the words of the famous prima donna, Clara Louise Kellogg, "the sound of those shuffling feet, shuffle, shuffle, shuffle — in the Court House grounds in Chicago: a sound like a great sea or forest in a wind as the people of the nation went in to look at their President whom they loved and who was dead."

There was also music, the German choirs of the city singing Bach and Handel, and a new song by George F. Root:

> Farewell Father, Friend and guardian,
> Thou has joined the martyrs' band;
> But thy glorious work remaineth,
> Our redeemed, beloved land.

"He was received with a solemn magnificence of pageantry and funeral pomp unexcelled anywhere," a local paper announced proudly. But the next day the city had one final tribute for its hero. To carry Lincoln's body and his grieving widow home to Springfield, Chicago brought forth George Pullman's resplendent Palace Car.

The City as Celebration

One of the chief functions of a city is to give a sense of celebration to the lives of its citizens and to visitors. Its streets should be avenues for the expression of moments of great national solemnity and rejoicing, as well as for the small passing delights of shopping and strolling. It must have places of worship in which to refresh the spirit and parks in which to refresh the body. The disappearance from our cities of this sense of celebration has cast a deep psychological pall over American life. Rarely now do we decorate our streets, open-air markets have all but vanished, and the exciting throngs of the downtown streets have been siphoned off to the drive-in shopping centers. As for our parks, on the whole poorly maintained, almost none now supply those pleasant, inexpensive places for dining and dancing that were once common to all.

PASSING SHOWS

Left: Abraham Lincoln's funeral cortege at Park Row. "At eleven o'clock on the morning of Monday, May 1, the funeral train reached Chicago, and here the mourning began to take on a character distinctly different from what had marked it in the East. The people who now met the coffin, who followed it to the court-house, who passed in endless streams by it to look at Lincoln's face, dated their trust in him many years earlier than 1861. Man after man of them had come to pay their tribute, not to the late President of the United States, but to the genial lawyer, the resourceful, witty political debater who had educated Illinois to believe that a country could not endure half slave and half free . . ." — Ida Tarbell, *Life of Lincoln.*

In the past, there were many ways for a city to celebrate
special events, such as the temporary structure, the Wigwam
(*above*), constructed especially for the 1860 Republican
convention which nominated Lincoln. Alexander Hesler's
photograph shows the building, at the corner of Lake
and Market Streets, while the convention was in session.
Afterward it was taken down.

Left, above: Triumphal arch on Michigan Avenue honoring the encampment of the
Grand Army of the Republic, August 31, 1900. The sculpture was the work of the
Chicagoan Lorado Taft. *Left, below:* World War I victory arch at the entrance to
Grant Park in 1918. The arch, with names of the battles in which Chicago dough-
boys took part, has been demolished. Its demise marked the end of the city's tradi-
tion of heroic street decoration.

Among the lost delights of the city are the special wagons
which plied their business in every byway. The Gay Nineties
musical evangelists (*above*) were not alone in mobilizing.
In his *Chicago Stories,* George Ade mentions the red wagons
of waffle men, buffet carts specializing in ham-and-egg
sandwiches, wheeled street pianos, mobile cobblers, carts
selling straw for bedding, lemonade, confectionery, pie, and
chewing-gum wagons, even a roving steam boiler to blow
out stopped-up pipes.

Flags and bunting were an always-popular form of marking
an event by, in a sense, putting new clothes on old buildings. *Right:* The Fair store on State Street, in full panoply
for President William McKinley in 1899.

The city did not neglect to note the springtime arrival of
its beloved White Stockings — later the White Sox. The
whimsical baseball player in living flowers (*right, below*)
grew on Drexel Boulevard in the 1890s.

PLACES OF WORSHIP

Trinity Episcopal Church (*left*), on Jackson Boulevard between Wabash and Michigan Avenues, was an excellent example of the pseudo-Gothic ecclesiastical edifices of the years just before the fire. It was consumed in 1871.

Originally built by Edward Burling and Dankmar Adler in 1875 and remodeled by Adler and Sullivan in 1892, Sinai Temple (*above*), at the southwest corner of Indiana Avenue and 21st Street, was a center of the German-Jewish Reform movement. It counted among its members Julius Rosenwald of Sears, Roebuck and Philip Dee Block of Inland Steel. The temple was demolished in the 1920s after the congregation had moved to South Shore.

St. Stanislaus Kostka (*left*), erected in the late 1870s on the southeast corner of Noble and Evergreen Streets, was the center of a West Side Polish community which once numbered 400,000. Much of that community has now moved to the suburbs, and the old church, showing signs of neglect, has lost one of its belfries so reminiscent of Cracow or Lodz.

Dwight L. Moody's Tabernacle (*below*), at La Salle Street and Chicago Avenue, was begun in 1873. The renowned evangelist, whose hymns such as "In the Sweet By and By" were the anthems of Victorian Protestantism, had his headquarters in Chicago until his death in 1899. His Tabernacle has vanished, but its spirit marches on at the Moody Memorial Church on Clark Street and North Avenue.

THE PLEASURE OF PARKS

A July Fourth celebration in the North Side's Lincoln Park in 1911 (*below*), an era when the activities of Chicago's parks were often aimed at familiarizing European immigrants with American traditions. In a tribute to Lincoln Park, George Ade said, "No Chicago millionaire has such a magnificent front yard."

"Drouet had taken three rooms, furnished, in Ogden Place, facing Union Park, on the West Side. That was a little, green-carpeted breathing spot, than which, today, there is nothing more beautiful in Chicago. It afforded a vista pleasant to contemplate. The best room looked out upon the lawn of the park . . . where a little lake lay sheltered." — Theodore Dreiser, *Sister Carrie*. Dreiser lived in a room overlooking Union Park (*above*) and this, with the spires of the Congregational Church in the background, is the view he described. Today, the park and its lovely lagoon are buried beneath a blanket of concrete.

Jackson Park on the lakefront was one of the three sites which Frederick Law Olmsted and his partner, Calvert Vaux, recommended to the city as recreation areas in 1871. The fire prevented them from carrying out their project at that time, but Olmsted later selected Jackson Park as the location for the 1893 Columbian Exposition. Afterward, it was transformed into one of Chicago's finest open spaces. This photograph, taken in the late 1890s, shows it after its transition from exposition ground to park. Jackson Park became the focus of the South Side's wealthiest communities. The hotels surrounding it — the Cooper-Carlton, the Sisson, the Flamingo, the Chicago Beach, and the Windermere — ranked with any in the city. Nearby South Shore Drive was lined with mansions and the South Shore Country Club was one of the most exclusive in Chicago. The park has suffered severely from the rapid deterioration of the surrounding neighborhoods. Most of the rich have moved away, the splendid hotels have either gone out of business or are struggling valiantly to maintain their old standards, and the South Shore Country Club closed its doors in the early 1970s.

Water — in the form of pools, formal basins, and Lake Michigan coves — provided one of the perpetual delights of Chicago's parks. *Above:* A Lincoln Park swan boat in 1899, and (*right*) the park's graceful iron bridge. Both the bridge and the swan boats have departed.

The architecture of park structures once gave untrammeled play to the imagination of the builders of America's cities. *Above:* The Club House of Washington Park Race Track in 1896, with the assembled members proudly posed. Proud they might be, for the 80-acre South Side track was one of the most imposing in the country. The work of Solon S. Beman, the builder of Pullman, its great day came with the annual running of the American Derby, Chicago's equivalent of the Kentucky Derby, the Preakness, and the Belmont. Old Washington Park passed out of existence in 1908. *Right, above:* A 1906 photograph of a fanciful lost pavilion on the beach at 78th Street. *Right, below:* The Municipal Pier, rechristened Navy Pier after the First World War, was constructed in 1916 as an easily accessible pleasure ground. Designed by Charles S. Frost, its three tiers jutting out into Lake Michigan offered a dance hall, theatre, restaurants, and an art gallery, topped by two graceful observation towers. The once-joyous structure now does duty as a warehouse.

STREETS FOR PEOPLE

Open-air markets, the delight of Americans abroad, flourished in our own cities in the nineteenth and early twentieth centuries. This is Maxwell Street's Jewish second-hand clothing mart around 1905, only one aspect of the varied ethnic mix of Chicago's West Side, described by Jane Addams, whose pioneering settlement was nearby, in *Twenty Years at Hull House:* "Between Halsted Street and the river live about ten thousand Italians . . . To the south of Twelfth Street are many Germans, and side streets are given over almost entirely to Polish and Russian Jews. Still farther south, these Jewish colonies merge into a huge Bohemian colony, so vast that Chicago ranks as the third Bohemian city in the world." The beginning of the end for many of the West Side neighborhoods came in 1957 with the Dan Ryan Express-way. The new Chicago Circle Campus of the University of Illinois did its best to finish the job in the mid-1960s, demolishing, among other things, most of Hull House.

South Water Street, paralleling the Chicago River, was the city's first thoroughfare.
Chicago, in a sense, grew up around it, and the South Water Street Market, seen
here in 1910, was, like Paris' Les Halles, the city's belly. The market was famed for
its fish, poultry, dairy products, and fruit; vegetables were sold in the Haymarket to
the west. But in the nineteenth century, when Chicago was the world's greatest
purveyor of game, its chief renown rested on its wild ducks, prairie chickens, and
snipe. The South Water Street Market closed in August of 1925, when its buildings
were replaced by a double-decked concrete highway reaching to the river's edge.
Even its historic name has disappeared, for it is now known as Wacker Drive.

". . . you take your life in your hand when you attempt the crossing of State Street, with its endless stream of rattling wagons and clanging trolley-cars," warned William Archer, the English author of *The Green Goddess*. By the time this photograph was taken, in 1907, State Street had fulfilled Potter Palmer's dream of making it one of the world's leading retail centers. No other city had so many famed department stores standing in such close proximity: Carson, Pirie, Scott; Mandel's; Rothschild's; The Fair; the Boston Store; Lytton's; Marshall Field. Starting in the 1960s, State Street began declining as a retail center and now many of its superb emporiums live only in memory.

"Get out of your train and drive up Michigan Avenue," the Chicago novelist Mary Borden exclaimed. "I defy you not to respond to the excitement in the air . . . not to throw your hat to the sky and shout. Beautiful! How beautiful it is as you whirl northward past the Tribune Tower . . ." In this view from Chicago Avenue in the 1920s, the new Gothic *Tribune* Tower, by Raymond Hood and John Meade Howells, rises in the distance on the left like a shimmering mirage, while on the right is the sparkling Wrigley Building. The open-top double-decker buses, which once offered for a nickel one of America's pleasantest rides, disappeared in the 1930s, another lost vehicle of celebration.

No single building's destruction in the Great Fire marked the passing of Old Chicago more dramatically than that of the Tremont House. This engraving, published within weeks of the conflagration, gives a highly accurate picture of the hostelry, which stood on the southeast corner of Lake and Dearborn Streets. The Tremont had roots going back to 1832, but the structure shown here is the 250-room building designed in 1850 by John Van Osdel. On July 9, 1858, Senator Stephen A. Douglas opened his re-election campaign on the Tremont's side balcony; the next day, his opponent, Abraham Lincoln, spoke from the same balcony. And it was at the Tremont, during his first visit to Chicago after the 1860 Republican convention, that Lincoln met his vice-presidential running mate, Hannibal Hamlin.

V

Holocaust

THE LATE SIXTIES continued the boom begun in the war years. With its population of 300,000 far outdistancing its old rivals St. Louis and Cincinnati, with only the long-established cities of the East selling more goods, with its exports exceeding $178 million a year, with its industrial development spreading south and west of the river, Chicago looked confidently to the future. Impressive mansions lined the well-paved streets of the North Side and, on the South Side, Prairie Avenue now began that progress toward opulence which would, in time, make it a rival of Philadelphia's Rittenhouse Square and New York's Fifth Avenue. The palatial emporium run by Field and Leiter on State Street was joined by an equally grandiose one under the aegis of Samuel Carson, John Pirie, and Robert Scott, while Peacock's had fresh competition in the sale of diamonds and rubies from S. Hoard & Company, which would one day become the elegant Spaulding's. Chicagoans liked to boast of the quality of education at the Rush Medical College, whose Dr. Daniel Brainard had been elected to the French Academy of Sciences, and to point out that the swing bridge designed by Newton Chapin and Daniel L. Wells had become a model throughout Europe. To top it all, the new Palmer House was, without doubt, to be counted among the finest hotels in the United States. One of its selling points was a telegraphic fire alarm in each room, a fire hose on each floor, and huge tanks of water on the roof.

The summer and autumn of 1871 had been exceptionally dry. Scarcely an inch of rain had fallen between July and October. All fall Chicago had been plagued by fires; a particularly serious one had occurred on October 7 at the Lull and Holmes planing mill on South Canal Street. Four blocks of modest frame dwellings had been destroyed before the blaze was finally brought under control. The ordeal had exhausted the city's fire department. The next day, a Sunday, a strong southwest wind had sprung up, parching the earth and drying the city even more. That night about nine o'clock, at the stable in the rear of the Patrick O'Leary house on De Koven Street on the far Southwest Side, an historic accident took place.

The usual form of the tale is that while Mrs. O'Leary was milking, her cow kicked over the kerosene lamp, thus setting fire to the hay in the barn. Though there can be little doubt that the O'Leary barn was where the fire started, the circumstances surrounding its beginning are difficult to ascertain. And certain questions must be asked. It seems a bit odd that a woman who milked her own cow every night would have placed a lantern in a position where the animal could easily kick it over. It also seems odd that most versions of the story say that the lantern was behind the cow when it was kicked over. Cows do not kick backward. There is one universally overlooked clue in all of the testimony surrounding this incident; that is Mrs. O'Leary's statement that there was an "explosion" when the lantern ignited the hay. A burning kerosene lamp does not explode. But that word may provide a solution to the mystery. At this time, long before the internal combustion engine, gasoline had almost no value, for it was merely that portion of raw petroleum which distilled off at a lower temperature than kerosene. It was usually thrown away. In the years before and after the Chicago fire, company after company was accused of adding gasoline to its kerosene, and one state after another passed legislation forbidding the practice. An "explosion"? Did Mrs. O'Leary's kerosene contain gasoline?

The blaze spread rapidly; the fire department was not notified for half an hour, and given that start and the high wind, the flames were already out of control before any apparatus arrived on the scene. At the Sherman House, Alexander Frear, a visiting politician from New York, was waiting for friends from Milwaukee. "There was a large crowd of strangers and businessmen of the city in the hotel," he remembered later. "The corridor and parlors were full of idlers, much as usual. While looking over the register some one said, 'There go the fire-bells again . . . They'll burn the city down if they keep on.'"

The strong wind drove the fire north, and within an hour the mills and furniture shops west of the river were ablaze and the flames began eating at the huge grain elevators along the bank. The homes of thousands of poor workers jammed in among the mills and shops were also consumed, and their terrified inhabitants fled north and east like refugees before a conquering army. Though by now the conflagration had attracted the attention of most of the city, in the more prosperous districts people still felt safe. The burned blocks of the previous night stood in the fire's path, creating what seemed like an impassable barrier, and beyond that was yet another wall, the vaunted fireproof stone edifices of the city's business district, the five- and six-story office buildings of Van Buren and Adams Streets.

At the gleaming new Palmer House, Mr. and Mrs. Alfred Hebard and their daughter were preparing for bed. They had stopped over in Chicago for a bit of shopping and sightseeing before proceeding home to Iowa after a visit back east. The Hebards heard that there was a big fire in the city, but there didn't seem to be any reason for concern. Didn't the Palmer House have those telegraphic fire alarms and those hoses and those tanks of water on the roof? But, as Mrs. Hebard remembered, they did want to have a look:

We immediately took the elevator to the upper story of the Palmer, saw the fire, but, deciding that it would not cross the river, descended to our rooms in the second story to prepare for sleep. Husband and daughter soon retired; I remained up to prepare for the morrow's journey, and thus gain a little time for shopping before the departure of the train at 11 a.m. Feeling somewhat uneasy, I frequently opened the blinds, and each time found the light in the streets increase until every spire and dome seemed illuminated.

The fire had leaped the wasteland left from the previous night and had been carried into the heart of the city by wind-blown pieces of burning wood which hurtled through the air like deadly missiles. Now graveled roofs and stone or cast-iron walls and alert watchmen counted for nothing. Aided by the blazing bridges and the fiercely flaming ships packed on the river for the annual fall sailings before the lake froze, the fire easily slipped within the gates at a hundred points. In a hot shower of light the tar works exploded, then the gas works, then the armory and the central police station. Like two arms of an invading host, the fire split, half heading east across Fifth Avenue and up La Salle, destroying the leading banks, the Board of Trade, and the most prestigious office buildings, while the other half moved north to devour the mansions on Monroe, Madison, and Washington streets. Above the shouts and screams of the panicked citizens, and the roar of the inferno could be heard the Court House bell, a dirge for a dying city.

Joseph Chamberlin, a twenty-six-year-old reporter for the *Evening Post,* tried to find out what his paper was doing about the fire:

When I crossed the river, I made a desperate attempt to reach my office on Madison Street beyond Clark. I pressed through the crowd on Randolph Street as far as La Salle, and stood in front of the burning Courthouse. The cupola was in full blaze, and presented a scene of the sublimest as well as most melancholy beauty.

Sweeping up La Salle, the flames destroyed the luxurious Grand Pacific Hotel and then turned on the Michigan Southern terminal. By now it was a fire storm, nearly white hot with very little smoke, lapping up oxygen like a dog lapping up water, an ancestor of those fire storms set off by World War II incendiary bombs in Hamburg and Dresden. In a desperate attempt to halt its progress, gunpowder was used to blow up buildings in its path, but to no avail. A grim gallows humor infected the dazed populace. "Chicago does nothing by halves," it was said, "not even its fires."

Northward the conflagration pressed, up Market Street and Wells and Franklin, burning the cheap buildings at the river end of Jackson, Quincy, and Adams. As it approached the Nevada Hotel, a popular rendezvous of visiting journalists and touring theatrical troupes, the manager had difficulty convincing some of the actresses, many of whom had just gone to bed, that the place was in danger. The burning wall next moved along South Water Street, consuming the lumber exchange and the densely clustered warehouses filled with millions of dollars' worth of French wine, Chinese tea, and Java coffee. At the lake end of the street, the Richmond House, where the Prince of Wales had stayed, and the Tremont both

quickly vanished. They were soon followed into oblivion by the Briggs and the Metropolitan. Nearby, dazzlingly new, was the half-million-dollar Bigelow House, its scheduled opening coinciding with the fire itself. Only the flames drank the contents of the already filled punchbowls standing on damask-covered tables in its dining room. And then it was the Sherman's turn. Alexander Frear reports that the fire suddenly was no longer a joking matter:

The corridor was a scene of intense excitement. The guests in the house were running about wildly, some of them dragging their trunks to the stairway. Everything was in confusion . . .

Soon the splendidly refurbished Crosby's Opera House went, and Hooley's, and the Field and Leiter store, and the newspapers: the *Evening Post,* the *Evening Mail,* the *Staats-Zeitung,* the *Tribune.* Eventually even the supposedly impregnable Palmer House was threatened. Mrs. Hebard had at last convinced her sleepy husband that he must do something:

Evidently the Palmer House was in great danger, and it was better to leave it now than to wait; but how to remove our baggage was the next question. Once we thought we had secured a cart or a wagon, but no sooner was the trunk thrown on than it was pulled off again by someone claiming a prior right . . .

The city was indeed in chaos. People staggered in the streets, drunk from the wares of the untended saloons; looting was rampant; children were lost; the main avenues were choked with treasures — paintings, pianos, mirrors, furniture — all carried a little way and then abandoned by their fleeing owners.

On Monday morning there was a rumor that the fire had been checked, but the story proved false. The flames leaped the river to the North Side and thirstily set to work first on the great breweries and then on the grand houses of Ohio and Rush and Cass and State Streets before turning on the churches: the New England and the Unity, Holy Name Cathedral and fashionable St. James'. Exhausted, despairing, Chicagoans stood by the thousands in the waters of Lake Michigan or huddled in the empty graves of the old cemetery north of the city which was being cleared to create Lincoln Park. Finally, about midnight on Monday, it began to rain. The flames died down; the

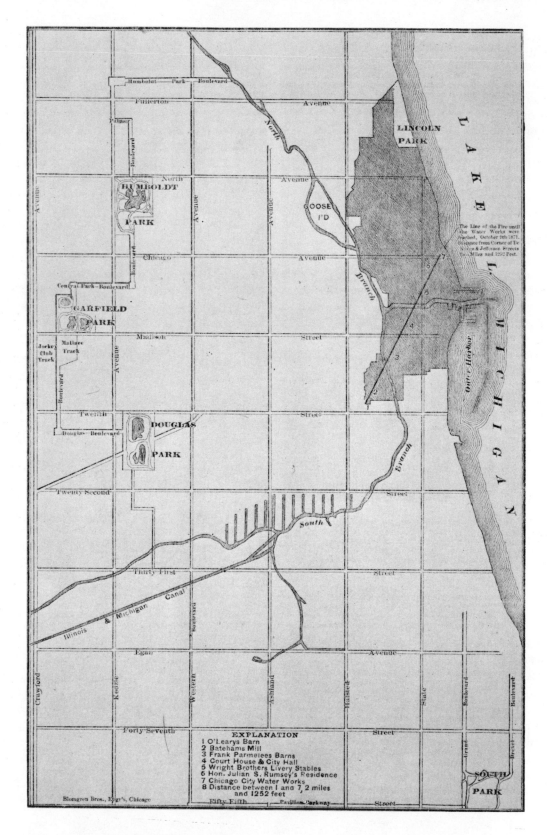

This map shows the area destroyed by the great fire of 1871 set against the city's later expansion. The burned district comprised the heart of Chicago, a region nearly four miles in length and almost two thirds of a mile wide.

embers ceased to glow. The Great Chicago Fire was history. The toll: three and a quarter square miles burned, 18,000 buildings destroyed, 100,000 persons homeless, 300 dead, more than $200 million in property lost. Certain irreplaceable things had been swept away: the Academy of Design, filled with paintings for an upcoming exhibition, the Chicago Historical Society, with Lincoln's own copy of the Emancipation Proclamation.

The prairie giant was, for a moment, as still as death. Bret Harte wrote a eulogy:

Blackened and bleeding, helpless, panting, prone
On the charred fragments of her shattered throne
Lies she who stood but yesterday alone.

Queen of the West! by some enchanter taught
To lift the glory of Aladdin's court,
Then lose the spell that all that wonder wrought.

Like her own prairies by some chance seed sown,
Like her own prairies in one brief day grown,
Like her own prairies in one fierce night mown.

The Chicago Fire

Certain disasters continue to linger in men's memories, held there either because of their drama or their magnitude. The names come quickly to mind: the San Francisco earthquake, the sinking of the *Titanic,* the *Hindenburg*'s destruction. The holocaust that swept over Chicago on October 9, 1871, is without doubt to be included among them. The statistics were indeed appalling. The fire burned a densely built-up urban area four miles long and two thirds of a mile wide, destroying property valued at more than $200 million. To those caught in its path, its power seemed almost satanic. In his *History of the Great Fires in Chicago and the West,* the Reverend Edgar J. Goodspeed of the Second Baptist Church wrote: "McVicker's Theatre and the *Tribune* building formed the northern boundary of [the fire] . . . it was here that the few workers now left with courage enough to contest with miserable fortune made their final stand. The *Tribune* building was believed to be fire-proof, if any structure devised by man could be proof against such a combination of the elements as was now raging. McVicker's yielded first, and was instantly a heap of brick and ashes, and the *Tribune* structure was not long in following."

Left: The ruins of the *Tribune* building, at the corner of Dearborn and Madison Streets. *Above:* The entrance to the Insurance Exchange on La Salle Street.

Above: A drawing of the palatial new Grand Pacific Hotel occupying the entire block bounded by Clark, Jackson, La Salle, and Quincy Streets. It was just preparing to open its doors when the fire struck.

Right: The gutted hotel after the flames had done their work. Its backers had at least one consolation: the Grand Pacific's ruins were considered the most impressive in the city.

Above: The burned Court House seen from the corner of Clark and Washington Streets. The nearest portion is one of the new wings Van Osdel added just before the fire.

Left: The ruins of the Honoré Building at Adams and Dearborn Streets, the property of Mrs. Potter Palmer's father.

"I remember driving downtown with my father through streets ragged and broken
. . . And everywhere around us, and northward as far as the eye could reach, nothing
but charred ruins, with only the castellated water tower rising intact high above the
ghostly devastation," wrote Harriet Monroe in *A Poet's Life*. The water tower, one
of the rare surviving structures in the city's burned district, became a symbol of
Chicago's will to survive, a striking example of the importance of historic landmarks
in the lives of people.

"Chicago may be taken as a fair type of American material energy. We are proud to claim her as a representative city, so far as vigor, boldness, self-poise, industry, and far-reaching enterprise are the characteristics of the American Republic . . . As Chicago was a representative city in the nation, so it shares in all the recuperative qualities of the Republic." — New York *Tribune* editorial shortly after the fire.

Chicago did indeed show amazing recuperative powers. Within days of the blaze, the Chamber of Commerce began clearing away the ruins of its old building and started construction of an even larger edifice, which was officially dedicated by Mayor Joseph Medill on the first anniversary of the fire. In this picture, taken in 1872 looking northeast from LaSalle and Madison Streets, workmen can be seen finishing the new Chamber's roof. The site is now occupied by the American National Bank Building.

VI
A Phoenix Rising

THE MORNING AFTER THE FIRE, Joseph Chamberlin witnessed an astonishing sight: "As I passed up West Madison Street, I met scores of working girls on their way 'down town' as usual, bearing their lunch-baskets, as if nothing had happened. They saw the fire and smoke before them, but could not believe the city, with their means of livelihood, had been swept away during the night."

It took days for Chicagoans to comprehend the full extent of the holocaust. Government officials, for instance, assumed that the currency stored in the Post Office and Custom House vaults had survived, protected by their three inches of boiler plate and a wall of brick. When, after four days, the smoking mass had cooled, it was discovered that the fire's 3000-degree heat had incinerated more than a million dollars. The story was the same at the city's banks. On Wednesday the *Tribune* published its first post-fire edition and its columns revealed the profoundly personal aspect of the tragedy:

Mrs. Bush is at 40 Arnold Street. She lost her baby. A little girl, cannot speak her name, at Desplaines Hotel. The wife and child of Rev. W. A. Jones are missing.

John Greenleaf Whittier expressed the consensus of an appalled nation:

On three score spires has sunset shone,
Where ghastly sunrise looked on none;
Men clasped each other's hands and said:
The City of the West is dead.

The obituary was premature. The keystone of Chicago's being, its island location, the prime reality which had allowed it to rise from a haunt of wolves to near greatness was still there. Its rich hinterland had not burned, nor had its lake, nor, above all, the bright rails reaching out to the Atlantic, the Pacific, and the Gulf. Many of its industries too had survived: the Union Stock Yards, 75 percent of its grain elevators, 80 percent of its lumberyards. Out on the West

Side stood more than 600 untouched factories. There was something else, too, something which in a later pretentiously unsentimental age, it is easy to discount: the city's spirit. In that first post-fire edition, the *Tribune* had extorted the citizens to "Cheer Up!"

In the midst of a calamity without parallel in the world's history, looking upon the ashes of thirty years accumulations, the people of this once beautiful city have resolved that CHICAGO SHALL RISE AGAIN!

Before the last coals had cooled, the marks of new life had appeared. Just days after the fire, the first commercial structure, a twelve-by-sixteen-foot shanty on Washington Street between Dearborn and Clark, was put up by W. D. Kerfoot, a leading real estate agent. The sign on the shanty was significant: "W. D. Kerfoot. Everything gone but Wife, Children and Energy." Field and Leiter soon opened for business in a carbarn. Chicagoans even found a constructive use for the ruins themselves. When they had ceased to smoke, the debris was pushed out into Lake Michigan to extend the city's shoreline. Today, under Grant Park's green lawns, a lost world lies buried.

The city's morale was helped immeasurably by an outpouring of sympathy and aid from the nation and the world. Louisville and Pittsburgh sent food. The city of Brooklyn and the New York Stock Exchange each pledged $100,000; A. T. Stewart, the dry-goods magnate, contributed $50,000 to be used exclusively for needy women. Money came from St. Louis and Cincinnati; from the hackmen of Washington, D.C.; from firms such as Morgan and the Rothschilds, from Canada, Germany, and France. The British donated 8000 books for a public library. Edwin Booth, Mrs. John Drew, and Charlotte Cushman all gave benefit performances. The Philadelphia Athletics played a benefit baseball game.

The help was desperately needed. Winter, the long, gray, brutal midwestern winter, was coming on, and in the city 100,000 were homeless and more than 35,000 faced starvation. The $1.98 worth of food distributed weekly to each needy family meant, in many cases, the difference between life and death. There was another matter, almost as urgent, that deeply concerned the thousands of unemployed: would the city's devastated industries rebuild? No industry was more basic to the city's economic welfare than the McCormick Company, whose $2 million plant lay in ruins.

Cyrus McCormick, already in his sixties, was known to be considering not rebuilding in Chicago and letting his other plants scattered across the country carry on his business. But when McCormick and his wife Nettie visited the rubble of his once-proud works, a moving, and perhaps decisive, demonstration took place. Cyrus McCormick had always been a popular employer, and now, as he walked amidst the twisted metal and piles of brick, the men cheered. Within three months a new McCormick Reaper Works had risen on Western Avenue.

Potter Palmer was in far more serious straits than was Cyrus McCormick. In a single night he had lost his magnificent new hotel, as well as the marble emporium he had constructed for Field and Leiter, and a mile of buildings on State Street. At the ripe age of forty-five he had just married the much-younger Berthe Honoré, the town's undisputed belle, and had looked forward to spending the rest of his life enjoying the good things of this world. Palmer was a man with a taste for the best: dining off vermeil, drinking champagne from crystal goblets, dashing about town in a four-horse barouche. Now, for the moment, all of that had to be put aside. Borrowing nearly $2 million from an insurance company — the largest loan ever made to an individual at that time — Palmer scoured the country buying materials to rebuild his beloved State Street. Day and night, by sunlight and arclight, the frantic work went on as his mercantile mile grew ever more splendorous. Its centerpiece was his new hotel. Using Van Osdel's plans for the lost building, Palmer had them greatly expanded to create one of the most sumptuous edifices in the United States.

That the post-fire Palmer House was the pre-fire Palmer House writ large, brings up an important point. Within six weeks after the fire, 318 permanent structures with a total frontage of three and one half miles had been begun. The sudden demand was so great that it was impossible for Chicago's architects to draw up original plans for every building, and many, following Palmer's lead, resurrected whatever blueprints they had salvaged and used them to reconstruct the city. It should not be surprising, therefore, that it is often difficult to distinguish buildings constructed just after the fire from those put up just before it.

Yet the hodgepodge of architectural styles that had marked the Chicago of the '60s was not to survive for long. In its place rose one supreme aesthetic ideal: the Paris of the Second Empire of Louis Napoleon and his empress, Eugénie. There had been elements of this taste in the Civil War city, but now, in the seventies, it swept aside most competitors. Louis Napoleon's political empire had already ceased to exist, destroyed in the debacle of the Franco-Prussian War of 1870, but his aesthetic empire had just begun its reign, surviving intact in the Paris created for him by the superb city planner Georges Haussmann. It was this, the Paris of grand boulevards, of the glittering new Opera House, of rich hotels and eye-catching department stores, that Chicago and all America now sought to emulate.

The midwife of this new taste was Richard Morris Hunt. As the first American architect to study at Paris' prestigious Ecole des Beaux-Arts, Hunt had written to his mother in 1855:

It has been presented to me that America was not ready for the fine arts, but I think they are mistaken. There is no place in the world where they are more needed, or where they should be more encouraged.

To Hunt, encouraging the fine arts meant encouraging the taste of Second Empire Paris. When he returned from his French sojourn, the young aesthetician was spectacularly prepared to carry out the task he had set for himself. He was a man of charm, a hard worker, and he was, without doubt, the best-trained architect in the United States. Above all, his timing was right. America's vast new fortunes, created by the Civil War and the enormous industrial expansion which followed, belonged to people who wished at once to express their bank balances and to legitimize them. Hunt now appeared to assure them that they were the new Medicis, and that therefore their lifestyle should be Medicean. He began by building a comparatively modest château on New York's Fifth Avenue for William K. Vanderbilt; later, for George Washington Vanderbilt, he would fabricate at Asheville, North Carolina, the largest house under one roof in America. Hunt's greatest triumph, though, would ultimately take place in Chicago.

Of all the city's architectural firms, none understood the Beaux Arts ideal better than Cudell and Blumenthal. Its senior partner, Adolph Cudell, a native of Germany, was responsible for Aldine Square on the South Side, an impressive post-fire achievement which, with its separate houses screened behind a handsome uniform façade, suggested a Parisian residential quarter. Cudell and Blumenthal's most spectacular commission was the mansion they designed in 1875 for Cyrus McCormick on Rush Street. An exuberant confection of columns, garlands, rusticated stonework, and crestings inspired by the Louvre's Pavillon Richelieu, it was truly a palace for a prince of industry.

It was not a residence, though, which would present the Beaux Arts style in all its panoply, but, rather, the new City and County Building. It would be easy to trace the whole history of taste in Chicago through its court houses, as they rose one after another, ever larger, ever grander, from the little temple of the first years, through Van Osdel's fine Greek Revival structure and his French wings, to the bedizened edifice that now became the seat of government for Chicago and Cook County. Three days after the fire, the City Council authorized the erection of a new court house. A competition for the project attracted some fifty designs, designs with names such as "Semper Resurgens" and "Legibus et Populis" and "In Hoc Signo Vinces." After this prodigal use of Latin, the council, in the best aldermanic tradition, announced that it had no qualified adviser to judge the entries and that, anyway, there had been no guarantee that the winner would get the job. It then promptly gave the commission to its personal favorite, James J. Egan, the county architect.

The vast building's walls and cost rose with equally astonishing extravagance. Standing on a tall two-story, cut-stone base, thirty-five-foot Corinthian columns of polished granite reached up to an elaborate entablature. Above that was an attic story embellished with allegorical groups representing Agriculture, Commerce, Peace, the Mechanic Arts, Science, and, for good measure, Plenty. Over it all was to loom a gigantic dome, but this final flourish was never attempted. The publicly announced cost of the structure was more than $4 million, and the council members did not occupy their palatial new chambers until 1885.

Long before that, in 1873 to be exact, Chicago felt itself sufficiently recovered to stage an Inter-State Industrial Exposition in the huge iron-and-glass hall William Boyington had constructed on Michigan Avenue. The exposition attracted thousands who wanted to see for themselves if "The City of the West" had been truly resuscitated. The signs of life were indisputable. From the genuine silver dollars paving the floor of the Palmer House's barber shop to the Grand Pacific's game dinners offering comestibles such as buffalo, antelope, bear, quail in plumage, and partridge in nest, the city's new hotels far surpassed those that had existed before Mrs. O'Leary's accident. McVicker's had reopened on its old site with a spectacular pinnacled building, and it now had stiff competition from Hooley's Theatre, which had been inaugurated in October 1872 with a bill that featured a pantomime, a Mardi Gras divertissement, and the Mademoiselles Elise and Marie Gratz giving "their Tyrolean eccentricities in song."

But for the discerning, the best show in town was not to be found at McVicker's or Hooley's or at any of the other dozen new theatres built in the post-fire years, but on the floor of the Chicago Board of Trade on La Salle Street. For now the dream of cornering the market took hold of men's minds, a dream tellingly dissected in Frank Norris' powerful novel of the Chicago Grain Exchange, *The Pit*. No one was more adept at getting a corner than Benjamin P. Hutchinson, "Old Hutch" as he was called on La Salle Street, who had arrived in Chicago as a bankrupt shoe manufacturer from Lynn, Massachusetts, and went on to found the Corn Exchange Bank. In 1888, Hutchinson cornered September wheat and made more than a million dollars in the process.

If the visitor was in town to shop, there was no place in the country quite like Field and Leiter's new store on State Street, which, with the withdrawal of Leiter in 1882, became officially Marshall Field's. Building on Potter Palmer's merchandising acumen, Field made his store the Midwest's supreme emporium. A trip to Chicago became synonymous with a visit to Field's. It was the dream of schoolgirls, the goal of brides, the happy memory of elderly ladies in all the little towns of the heartland. At Field's one could find gowns like those designed in Paris by Monsieur Worth, the rarest of veilings, Oriental rugs made by special order in Persia to fit the size and shape of a modern house. In 1872 sales totaled $3 million; ten years later the firm was doing an annual business in excess of $24 million.

There was one place that was always at the top of any Chicago visitor's sightseeing list: the Union Stock Yards. In the years since the Civil War, Morris and Company had been joined by Swift, Armour, and Cudahy, and together they made up the Big Four which shared among themselves most of Chicago's meat packing. There was a good deal to share. Incoming hogs alone increased from three million in 1872, to five million in 1882, to seven million in 1892, and the number of cattle and sheep soared proportionately. More than any other industry, the Yards exported the name Chicago around the world. By the late '70s, the packers had perfected the canning of meat — corned beef, roast beef, ox tongue, potted ham — and in the golden age of empire building, this Chicago invention became a necessity for European countries with armies in tropical climes. During the 1883 Sudan expedition against the Mahdi, the British government ordered no less than 740,000 pounds of Chicago beef, an order expanded the next year to 2,500,000 pounds. The event was noted by an anonymous rhymster:

> *The roast beef of Old England*
> *Is famed in song and story,*
> *Without it where was English brawn*
> *That won old England glory?*
>
> *But in these days of England's gloom,*
> *When war's dread notes alarm her,*
> *What does she send to save Khartoum?*
> *Corned beef canned by Phil Armour.*

Around the great packing houses, an almost self-sufficient town grew up — "Back-of-the-Yards," as it was called. Here, in row upon row of dilapidated wooden houses the workers lived: first Germans, then Irish, then Poles, Czechs, and finally, Lithuanians. At the turn of the century, Upton Sinclair's vivid portrait of their stunted lives in *The Jungle* would arouse an entire nation.

There was another company town in Chicago. The use of The Pioneer to carry Lincoln's body back to Springfield had sparked a rage for sleeping cars, and George Pullman rapidly expanded his hold on the market, not only by the excellence of his product and services, but by buying out his competitors. By 1890 the Pullman Company was carrying nearly five million passengers a year, offering such luxurious innovations as steam heat, electric lights, and separate toilets for men and women. It even had a company song:

> *Hurrah for a ride without jostle or jar!*
> *Hurrah for a life on the iron bar!*
> *Hurrah for a ride in a Pullman car!*
> Vive la compagnie!

As a monument to his success, the sleeping car magnate built in 1882, on the South Side near 111th Street, America's most spectacular privately owned city. Designed by Solon S. Beman, one of Chicago's most inventive architects, Pullman was modeled on the Krupp complex near Essen, Germany. Here, in a perfectly planned community, George Pullman offered his employees a shopping arcade, a theatre, a library, a hotel, and decent housing, all in an attractive park-like setting. The idea was good, the execution brilliant, but the continuing company ownership of the workers' houses bore the seeds of a terrible conflict.

It was indeed an impressive Chicago which rose in the dozen years after the fire. The city, all agreed, was the fastest growing metropolis in the world; with its population already more than 500,000, there were those who predicted that in another decade it would reach a million. Lady Duffus Hardy, who had made a splash with a string of best-selling novels including *Beryl Fortescue* and *Paul Wynter's Sacrifice,* had expected, when she paid a visit in the '80s, to find the Chicagoans still living among ruins. The reality surprised her:

Knowing of the fiery scourge which a few years ago had marred and scarred the beauty of that fair city, we expected to find traces of ugliness and deformity everywhere . . . But, Phoenixlike, the city has risen up out of its own ashes, grander and statelier than ever.

The Grand Hotels

Chicago's hotels had both a national and an international reputation for size and luxury, but they held a very special place in the hearts of Midwesterners. It was probably a Chicago hotel that figured in the honeymoon, in that all-important business trip, in the memorable excursion to the Columbian Exposition of 1893 or the Century of Progress of 1933. Due to the city's role as America's favorite political convention site, its hotels also had a place in history. It was the Blackstone which supplied the "smoke-filled room" where, in 1920, Warren Gamaliel Harding was chosen as the Presidential standard-bearer of the Grand Old Party.

The beginnings of the Chicago hotel lay in small establishments such as the Green Tree Inn (*below*), built by James Kinzie at the corner of Canal and Lake Streets in 1833. The Green Tree was later moved to Milwaukee Avenue, where it stood when George Ade visited it in the 1890s. Ade was touched by the old building, which he said was the only one in the city that an officer from Fort Dearborn would recognize. "He would find the same old roof, the same square-paned little windows and the clapboarded walls growing rusty in spite of repeated paintings." When this photograph was taken in 1901, the group shown was trying to save the structure. Their efforts were in vain. The next year Chicago's oldest landmark was razed.

Typical of the large pre-fire hotels was the Briggs House (*above*) designed by John Van Osdel and constructed in 1856 at the northeast corner of Wells and Randolph Streets. Its lobby windows were handsome examples of the arched Victorian style which replaced the more severe square-topped windows of the Greek Revival. The Briggs was one of the large downtown buildings lifted a full story (*left*) in 1857 after the city's street grade was raised. The hotel was a victim of the **Great Fire**.

Right: The Union Stock Yards, located between 39th and 47th Streets and Ashland Avenue and Halsted Street, were a city unto themselves. Their town hall was the Exchange Building seen on the left. When this photograph was taken in 1905, the Yards employed 75,000 workers, supported another 250,000 people in their immediate neighborhood, received some 17 million animals, and processed $500 million worth of meat products annually.

The Yards even had their own hotel, the Transit House (*above*), built in 1869. Here, in the lush days, cowboys and cattlemen from the West mixed with purchasing agents for the armies of the German and French and British empires and with the princes of Packingtown — Nelson Morris, Gustavus Swift, and Philip D. Armour. The Transit House burned in 1912 and was replaced by the Stock Yards Inn. With the shift of meat packing to cities other than Chicago, the Yards themselves became, in 1971, a lost legend.

"There is over a square mile of space in the yards, and more than half of it is occupied by cattle pens; north and south as far as the eye can reach there stretches a sea of pens."
— Upton Sinclair, *The Jungle*.

The Sherman House, named for its owner, Francis C. Sherman, the city's Civil War mayor, had one of the longest runs of any Chicago hotel. The first was built in 1845; the second (*above*), constructed on the original site at Clark and Randolph Streets, was designed by William W. Boyington in 1861. When it was destroyed in the fire, Boyington was called back to design its successor (*below*), which survived until 1910. The fourth Sherman House (*right, above*) was the work of the distinguished firm of Holabird and Roche. Its owner, Ernie Byfield, made its College Inn a gathering place for show people and the headquarters of Chicago's favorite band leader, Isham Jones. The ballroom of the Sherman in 1914 (*right, below*), with the goateed Buffalo Bill on the right. The Sherman House closed its doors in 1973.

Supreme among the post-fire hotels was the $2,500,000 Palmer House at State and Monroe Streets. The design of the hotel was based on plans by John Van Osdel which were expanded by C. M. Palmer, an architect who did much work in Chicago in the 1870s. The Palmer House gloried in thirty-four varieties of marble, a twenty-five-foot-high rotunda, an Egyptian parlor, and furniture imported from France and Italy. It also claimed to be the world's first fireproof hotel — a strong selling point in Chicago — and 600 tons of Belgium iron was used in its construction. This Palmer House was demolished in 1925 to make way for the current hotel of that name.

The Palmer House's Grand Dining Room, 64 feet wide and 76 feet long, was enriched with gilded Corinthian columns, a marble floor, and frescoes painted by Italian artists. The damask table linen was made especially for the hotel in Belfast. The room was the scene of a spectacular banquet for Ulysses S. Grant in 1879, featuring Mark Twain as speaker and a game dinner of saddle of venison, roast prairie chicken, buffalo steak, breast of duck, and filet of wild turkey.

The Windermere West, shown here in 1905, at 56th Street and Cornell Avenue, was one of the gracious residential hotels of the South Side. It was part of that quarter's vanished world which included Aldine Square, Prairie Avenue, and Drexel and Grand Boulevards. The old hotel, with its white verandahs so reminiscent of southern resorts, was superseded in the 1920s by the new Windermere East, overlooking Jackson Park at 56th Street and East End Avenue.

"I read Letty my new contribution to the *Little Review* before offering it to its high priestess. The reading took place in the Blue Fountain Room . . . where a single meal meant bankruptcy." — Ben Hecht, *Gaily, Gaily*.

Above: A corner of the Blue Fountain Room in the La Salle Hotel, constructed by Holabird and Roche on La Salle Street in 1908. The room, a favorite gathering place of the more affluent among the writers who flourished in Chicago before the First World War, had been remodeled beyond recognition by the time the hotel was razed in 1977.

The Silver Forest Room (*right*) was the showplace of Marshall and Fox's Drake Hotel of 1921. It was used for dining and for dancing to the music of Hal Kemp, Jack Hilton, and Alec Templeton, as well as for the reception of visiting dignitaries such as Queen Marie of Rumania. The Drake is still a North Michigan Avenue landmark, but the Silver Forest's sumptuous space has been parceled out among several smaller rooms.

"Most of the panes that enclosed this central space were of great height and breadth ... others, smaller, gave light and some ventilation." — Henry B. Fuller, *The Cliff-Dwellers*. The novelist Fuller coined the now-famous phrase "cliff-dwellers" to describe the office workers in the pre-eminent early Chicago skyscraper, the Rookery. Its great lobby, shown here shortly after completion in 1886, was one of the Chicago School's most dynamic interiors. The building, on South La Salle Street, is still standing, one of three survivors out of a total of twenty-seven by Burnham and Root which once graced the Loop. The lobby, though, was considerably changed during a 1904 modernization by Frank Lloyd Wright. At that time its delightful Art Nouveau lighting fixtures were replaced by massive planters and part of its daring expanse of glass was covered, thus lessening its exuberant aviary quality.

VII

An Architecture for a Democracy

Louis Sullivan concludes his essay "The Tall Office Building Artistically Considered" with these words:

. . . when we know and feel that Nature is our friend, not our implacable enemy . . . then it may be proclaimed that we are on the high-road to a natural and satisfying art, an architecture that will soon become a fine art in the true, the best sense of the word, an art that will live because it will be of the people, for the people, and by the people.

That the words of the supreme architect of the heartland should echo the words of its supreme statesman is no coincidence. The same forces that shaped the man who saved the republic and who proclaimed, "As I would not be a slave, so I would not be a master" made Chicago the natural site of America's first school of democratic architecture. They were the forces that would make the heartland the seedbed of America's realistic literature and transform our speech

from the tight circumscribed tongue of England into the broad expression of a vast continent. In *The American Language*, H. L. Mencken saw it all beginning with Chicago's first hero, Andrew Jackson:

. . . it was his fate to give a new and unshakable confidence . . . at the Battle of New Orleans. Thereafter all doubts began to die out; the new Republic was turning out a success . . . The hordes of pioneers rolled down the Western valleys and on to the great plains. America began to stand for something quite new in the world — in government, in law, in public and private morals, in customs and habits of mind, in the minutiae of social intercourse.

Chicago, the most American of cities, was at the center of this new creation. It was not surprising, therefore, that here were felt the first stirrings of a native architecture which was not provincial, not colonial, which proudly asserted the United States' aesthetic independence by at last breaking with European precedents. As Pullman and McCormick had changed America, as Lincoln had, now came men who would transform its very appearance: William Le Baron Jenney, Dankmar Adler, Louis Sullivan, John Wellborn Root, Frank Lloyd Wright. The architectural historian James Marston Fitch, in his *American Building,* gives this explanation:

These men developed in the electric environment of a vigorous and progressive capital, intellectual center of the Midwest. In the older cities of the eastern seaboard, the Wall Street capitalists had already consolidated their power and settled down for a long period of intensifying conservatism. Chicago, on the other hand, was the pivot of industrial and agrarian forces which resisted, for the time at least, the long arm of eastern monopoly. It faced huge new problems and had no choice but to try new solutions.

The problems or, better, the challenges were indeed huge. Travelers noted an actual hum as they approached Chicago.. "Conceive a city all [of] whose principal streets correspond to Victoria Street in London, or the most central parts of Glasgow and Manchester," an Englishman, Sir John Leng, wrote in the mid '70s, "and you will understand the style of the Chicago of to-day." Seventy-five passenger trains now served it daily, while its port annually cleared more than 10,000 vessels. In the two decades after the fire the value of construction amounted to more than $300 million and by 1890 land in the Loop (so named because of the loop made first by cable cars and later by the elevated around the city's business section) was selling for $900,000 a quarter-acre.

Hard pressed to keep up with the demand, Chicago's builders invented one revolutionary method of construction after another. Salt was added to mortar so that bricks could be laid in winter; lights were placed under temporary roofing to permit excavation at any time and in any weather; straw was packed around concrete so that it could be poured even in a blizzard. But it was left to William Le Baron Jenney, an engineer who had graduated from the Ecole Centrale des Arts et Manufactures in Paris and who had built bridges for the Union army, to come up with the most profound innovation of all. In 1884, at the corner of Dearborn and Washington Streets, Jenney constructed for the Home Insurance Company the world's first iron-and-steel-framed building. After that it was possible to reach up to almost any height, to do away with thick stone or brick supporting walls and to replace them with thin curtain walls which could be cut away to permit larger and larger windows. Though it would take time for the full implication of the Home Insurance Building to be understood, Jenney had prefigured the skyscraper and the all-glass tower.

Major Jenney's office was one of the most important training grounds for the architects of the Chicago School. Through it passed Martin Roche and William Holabird, who would team up to found a distinguished architectural firm of their own; Irving K. Pond, James Gamble Rogers, Alfred Granger, Howard Van Doren Shaw, and to this office in 1873 came the most famous of them all, Louis Henri Sullivan. After training at the Massachusetts Institute of Technology in his native state and a stint in a Philadelphia architect's office, Sullivan was searching for a larger field of action, and when he saw Chicago he knew that he had found it. In his *The Autobiography of an Idea,* a book which ranks with *The Education of Henry Adams* as one of the most profound self-revelatory works in American literature, Sullivan recorded his first emotions toward the city of his destiny:

Louis thought it all magnificent and wild: A crude extravaganza: An intoxicating rawness: A sense of big things to be done.

The Jenney atelier was a congenial place for a bright, energetic young man. Not only was the Major a fine teacher, but he was also a delightful human being. Sullivan was to remember him as "a *bon vivant,* a gourmet" who "knew his vintages, every one." Because he felt it important for an architect to experience the good things of life, Jenney encouraged his staff to go to the theatre, to restaurants, to concerts, and, above all, to the beer gardens the Germans had introduced into the city which gave it a surprisingly continental air. Scattered across town, from Henry Schoelkopf's Relic House on the North Side to Baum's Pavillion on the South, they offered wine and beer, Viener schnitzel and sauerbraten, good orchestras, and, often on Sunday afternoons, operetta.

Sullivan's guide to this new world was Jenney's foreman, John Edelmann, an enthusiastic, well-read young man of twenty-four. Edelmann introduced Sullivan to the progressive political theories that were swirling about the Middle West — the single tax, and the need for an exclusively greenback currency — and to German metaphysics and books such as Charles Darwin's *On the Origin of Species* which would profoundly influence his architectural theories. On Sundays Edelmann and Sullivan went to Turner Hall on the North Side to hear Hans Balatka's orchestra perform Wagner, then the musical rage. A passion for serious music seems to have been common to almost all of the architects of the Chicago School. It was a passion easily satisfied in a city boasting a symphony under the brilliant baton of the German-born conductor Theodore Thomas, as well as the Bush Temple of Music with its fine conservatory and the Chicago Musical College, presided over by the popular Dr. Florenz Ziegfeld, whose son would one day employ melody to glorify the American girl.

This *joie de vivre* shared by Jenney, Edelmann, Sullivan, and the other members of the Chicago School is an important factor in understanding their architecture. It was a natural element in a metropolis without a strong Puritan tradition, which from its beginnings delighted in plays, music, and dancing. It is significant that the consummate expressions of the School were to be office buildings, hotels, concert halls, cafes, beer gardens, and theatres. It was to be a supremely public architecture, an enhancement of places where the people gathered.

It was because of this awareness of the people as equal citizens of a republic — an awareness as profound as that felt by Lincoln himself — that the Chicago architects wanted buildings which would reflect the political and economic realities of the United States. The Chicagoans were not satisfied merely to build structurally innovative edifices; they wanted them to be stylistically, revolutionary as well. They sought reality, not fantasy, and the reality of America as seen from the heartland did not include the pavilions of princes or the castles of kings. Sullivan's colleagues agreed with him when he called pseudo-Gothic churches and ersatz Palladian office buildings mere "architectural theology." They found their inspiration not in the Venice of the doges, or in the Rome of the Caesars, or in the Paris of the Bonapartes, but in Joseph Paxton's Crystal Palace in London, John Roebling's Brooklyn Bridge, and the new fireproof Chicago warehouses of George H. Johnson and Freder-

ick Baumann. Here were no Philadelphia waterworks disguised as Greek temples, no Hartford, Connecticut, firearms factory pretending to be an Oriental seraglio. Sullivan, the chief theorist of the Chicago School, would call for buildings where "form followed function," just as it had in the sanctuaries of ancient Greece and in the twelfth-century Gothic cathedrals. He would call for a decoration based, not upon the copybooks in the university libraries, but on natural forms, the living reality of the American land. And always, at the very heart, was the belief that architecture must celebrate its own time and that this time was one of technology, industry, and, above all, democracy. The Roman temple had no place in our cities. To use it as the form of a bank, he would write later in his *Kindergarten Chats*, was as ridiculous as requiring a banker to "wear a toga." Elsewhere in the *Chats*, in a passage suggesting Gertrude Stein's "A rose is a rose is a rose," Sullivan reiterated why our architecture must be American:

Furthermore, if the pseudo-Roman temple were good for any one thing in America, it must, ipso facto, be good for anything and everything American, because American means American, and expresses the genius of the people. But Roman does not mean American, never did mean American. Roman was Roman; America is, and is to be, American.

This was the authentic voice of the heartland.

Sullivan was not the only Chicago architect deeply concerned with perfecting an American stylistic theory. John Wellborn Root was another. Born in Georgia, educated in England and in New York as a civil engineer, Root had worked in the office of James Renwick, the architect of the Smithsonian Institution in Washington. After arriving in Chicago in 1871, he linked up with Daniel Burnham, who had come to architecture by way of selling plate glass and mining and who had one consuming ambition: to be a millionaire. Their first important commission, in 1874, was for a house on Prairie Avenue for John B. Sherman, "the father of the Yards." Of pressed brick and sandstone, its strong, simple lines stood out in sharp contrast to the convoluted Beaux Arts palaces surrounding it. In 1882 Burnham and Root carried the aesthetic ideals of the Sherman residence into the commercial world with their Montauk Block, where, within the very shadow of the Parisian grandeur of the Palmer House, the young architects put up an unadorned nine-story brick structure which proclaimed proudly that it was nothing more and nothing less than an office building.

The startlingly straightforward elevations of the Montauk Block were no accident. In the '80s, Root had begun writing for Chicago's progressive building journal, the *Inland Architect,* a series of pioneering essays which expressed concepts given form in both the Sherman residence and the Montauk Block:

We must especially beware of the servile imitation of those greatest and completest styles that mark the end of long periods of architectural development.

And:

As far as material conditions permit it to be possible, a building designated for a particular purpose should express that purpose in every part.

Because Root was to die at forty, it would be Louis Sullivan who would give final form to these ideals.

By the time Sullivan met the man who would be his partner in accomplishing this task, he had spent a frustrating term at the Ecole des Beaux Arts which had deepened his conviction that the architectural solutions for America did not lie in Europe. The introduction came through his old friend John Edelmann. "Further away stood Adler at a draftsman's table," Sullivan was to write. "He was . . . heavy-set, well-bearded, with a magnificent domed forehead which stopped suddenly at a solid mass of black hair." Dankmar Adler was the son of a German Jewish rabbi and cantor who for more than thirty years was the spiritual leader of Chicago's prestigious Anshe Mayriv congregation. After serving, like Jenney, as an engineer in the Union army, he had formed a partnership with Edward Burling, and, in the years after the fire, Burling and Adler were responsible for more than a hundred buildings in Chicago, including the *Tribune* offices, Delmonico's restaurant, and the Methodist Church Block.

Adler was both popular and successful and, in 1879, encouraged by the commission to design the important Central Music Hall at the corner of State and Randolph Streets, he decided to go into business for himself. Needing a draftsman, he hired Louis Sullivan, whose first task was to design the new hall's organ grilles. The Central Music Hall was the prototype of the kind of theatre that would make Adler and Sullivan famous, an effective combination of shops, offices, and an auditorium with perfect acoustics. Indeed, Adler was the greatest acoustical engineer of his time, with a knowledge of sound unique in the nineteenth century. He was responsible for the splendid acoustics of the Chicago theatres — such as the Schiller — he and Sullivan built, as well as those of New York's Carnegie Hall.

It was Adler and Sullivan's skill in designing theatres that brought them their greatest commission. After hosting the 1880 and 1884 Republican conventions, the barnlike Inter-State Exposition building on the lakefront had stood empty for months. Ferdinand Peck, heir to a large Chicago real estate fortune and a serious patron of music, conceived the idea of using the building for a summer festival featuring Theodore Thomas' orchestra. Adler was asked to convert the cavernous interior into a concert hall, and the ingenious plan he devised not only provided seats for 6000 but also enabled all to hear each instrument distinctly. The success of the festival led Peck to begin thinking of a permanent concert hall on a grand scale, and who could better design it than Adler and Sullivan?

In 1886, when the Auditorium commission came to them, Adler was forty-two and Sullivan thirty. They were at the height of their powers and they would need all of their strength and skill for the monumental job ahead of them. Fortunately they had a staff of unusual talent. There was George Elmslie, who would design some of the most glorious small buildings of the twentieth century; Paul Mueller, a brilliant construction engineer who would share the honors for Tokyo's Imperial Hotel; and a young man still in his teens, Frank Lloyd Wright.

Sullivan's first designs show a picturesque structure complete with oriel windows, a high gable roof, dormers, and pinnacles. But nearby was rising Henry Hobson Richardson's Marshall Field Wholesale Store, and it was an unmistakable lesson in how a modern building should look. Richardson was the one eastern architect unreservedly admired by the men of the Chicago School. His Trinity Church in Boston, his Ames Memorial Library in North Easton, Massachusetts, his Allegheny County buildings in Pittsburgh were all impressive examples of a virile, modified Romanesque style. The final and most complete statement of that style was his building for Marshall Field. A solid block of masonry-supporting walls, it was stripped of almost all decoration, achieving its breathtaking beauty by means of fine workmanship and the powerful rhythms of its window openings: uniform for the first two floors, doubled for the upper two, quadrupled in the attic. Years later, in his *Kindergarten Chats,* Sullivan was to call the Field building "this oasis in our desert"; now he was to learn from it. Leveling gables and pinnacles and dormers, Sullivan sketched a simplified lithic structure with but a single, massive tower.

From the moment in 1887 when President Grover Cleveland laid the cornerstone of the Auditorium, Chicago sensed that it was a very special building. In the first place, the effort required for its construction reminded observers of the pyramids. At its acre-and-a-half site on Michigan Avenue at Congress Street, two hundred men and thirty teams of horses labored day and night digging a stupendous pit for its foundations. These consisted of an ingenious floating network of huge timbers, steel rails, and iron I-beams strong enough to support the 4000 pounds per square foot pressed down upon them by the massive load-bearing walls of Indiana limestone and Minnesota granite. To insure that the seventeen-story tower, which alone weighed 15,000 tons, would settle at the same rate as the rest of the building and thus not crack the walls, Adler devised a brilliant mathematical formula which allowed him to load the lower floors artificially and then gradually empty them as they rose above the main body of the structure. The Auditorium Tower immediately became the city's leading tourist attraction — Chicago's equivalent of the dome of St. Paul's in London — the place where all went to view this astonishing prairieland capital. Paul Bourget, a French novelist, found it like nothing else in the world: "It is two hundred and seventy feet high, and it crowns and dominates a cyclopean structure which connects a colossal hotel with a colossal theatre."

"Colossal" was indeed the word heard time and again when, on December 9, 1889, President Benjamin Harrison dedicated the Auditorium. (The packed house — many of whom had paid $2000 for a box seat — not only got to see the President, but also heard the soprano Adelina Patti, sing "Home, Sweet Home.") And colossal was an accurate description, for the Auditorium Theatre, seating 4000 with room for another 3000 on special occasions, was the largest opera house in the world. Its enormous orchestra pit could hold 110 musicians, and the stage could be extended out over the parquet to form the nation's biggest ballroom. Yet Adler had made its acoustics so perfect that every word of a conversation on its mammoth stage could be heard with ease in the top gallery, some six stories up and half a block away. The structure was rich in innovations. It was the first new building in the world to be electrically lit, and enormous fans, drawing air down shafts from the roof and forcing it through sprays of water and over blocks of ice, made it the first to be air-conditioned.

There was another word which was often heard that December night: beautiful. In the decoration of the interior, Sullivan proved beyond doubt that architects need not look to Greece or Rome or the Middle Ages in order to create beauty. The forms based on nature, which he so strongly advocated, were more than sufficient. The theatre ceiling was a series of sweeping gold-leaf-covered arches set with diamondlike, carbon-filament lights. The effect was to crown every citizen of the republic at every performance with an equally brilliant tiara. Sullivan's genius was evident in all aspects of the building's decoration: in the subtle variations of the ivory and gold stenciling on the walls, in the carpets and iron work, in the designs of the fifty million tesserae which made up the mosaic floors. But in the Auditorium's long bar, Sullivan surpassed himself, and in so doing he made artistic history. Here he gave his theories of decoration untrammeled play and enriched the room's ceiling and columns with a wondrous foliate flowering like nothing the world had ever seen before. By that act Louis Sullivan's fertile imagination had created Art Nouveau, the style that was to dominate the end of the century. In *The Roots of Modern Design,* Sir Nikolaus Pevsner, the English art historian, gives Sullivan his due:

The two creators of Art Nouveau were Louis Sullivan in Chicago and Victor Horta in Brussels. Sullivan was probably essentially original . . . By the time Sullivan designed the interiors of the Auditorium Building in Chicago, this is by 1888, his ornamental style was complete.

The Auditorium was an unqualified success from the moment it opened. Adler and Sullivan moved their offices into the tower, the hotel at once joined the august company of the Palmer House, the Sherman, and the Grand Pacific, its restaurants and banqueting rooms became the gathering places of the city's fashionable; but it was the theatre which was its glory. To it came Enrico Caruso, Amelita Galli-Curci, John McCormick, Luisa Tetrazzini, and Dame Nellie Melba, who said, "I wish I could fold it up and take it with me everywhere." Richard Strauss, Sergei Prokofiev, and Nikolai Rimsky-Korsakov all conducted there. On its stage Booker T. Washington and President McKinley made their joint appeal for racial tolerance, Theodore Roosevelt launched his Bull Moose campaign, and Will Rogers first found fame for his heartland humor. Near the end of his life, Frank Lloyd Wright reminisced about working there for the two geniuses whose monument it will always be, and called it "the greatest room for music and opera in the world."

The Auditorium was indeed an extraordinary building, perhaps the most extraordinary ever constructed in America, but suddenly Chicago was full of remarkable buildings, all reaching up as high as their load-bearing walls would carry them. This desperate race for height was the result of a combination of a continuing boom and the extreme restriction of the city's central business district. Bound on the north and west by the Chicago River, on the south by an impassable network of railroads and on the east by Lake Michigan, its total area was barely three quarters of a square mile. The only direction to go was up. The architects who first accomplished this feat with a high degree of perfection were undoubtedly Burnham and Root. Their Rookery of 1885, at the southeast corner of La Salle and Adams streets in the heart of the financial district, set a standard for office size, width of corridors, and placement of elevators which was to be followed in commercial buildings for fifty years; while the three-story entrance court of glass and iron was one of the Chicago School's finest interiors. Burnham and Root matched this triumph with their awesomely sophisticated sixteen-story Monadnock Building on West Jackson Boulevard. In subtle tribute to the city which gave it life, the Monadnock's severe, Egyptian-inspired walls flared out at base and parapet to form the silhouette of a growing papyrus or of its relative, the wild onion.

The Monadnock was at once the supreme load-bearing wall skyscraper and the last. By the time it opened in 1892, the Chicago architects had mastered all the lessons of Major Jenney's Home Insurance Building. William Holabird and Martin Roche not only used an iron-and-steel frame for their handsome Tacoma, but also introduced the idea of riveting it into place, thus greatly reducing the time it took to construct a build-

ing. Soon, Holabird and Roche were dotting the Loop with their distinctive structures: the Caxton, the Pontiac, the Old Colony, the splendid Marquette. Chicago now became a forest of true skyscrapers, their iron-and-steel trunks growing upward toward the dizzying height of twenty stories. There was the Chamber of Commerce by Baumann and Huehl; the Manhattan by the still-active Le Baron Jenney; and Adler and Sullivan's exquisitely decorated Stock Exchange. Standing on top of the Auditorium Tower, Paul Bourget was awed:

It needs but a few minutes for the eyes to become accustomed to the strange scene. Then you discern differences of height among these levels. Those of only six or seven stories seem to be the merest cottages, those of two stories are not to be distinguished from the pavement, while the "buildings" of fourteen, fifteen, twenty stories, uprise like the islands of the Cyclades as seen from the mountains of Negroponte.

Again it was a Burnham and Root building that focused the attention of America and Europe on the Chicago skyscraper. Everything about their Masonic Temple of 1892 on the northeast corner of State and Randolph streets was worthy of a superlative. At twenty-two stories it was by far the tallest building in the world. Its basement restaurant seated 2000, its interior shopping galleries were huge, its elevators numbered fourteen, its roof garden rested literally in the clouds. During the 1893 Columbian Exposition, knowledgeable European visitors turned their backs on the fair's imitative architecture and asked to see the Masonic Temple. Along with Adler and Sullivan's Wainwright Building, constructed in St. Louis at the same time, the Temple — with its distinct base, its soaring shaft uninterrupted by horizontal divisions, and its fine functional cape — gave the basic form to the powerful skyscrapers of the '90s.

With such buildings the Chicagoans frankly and joyously celebrated the life of the new industrial age about them. Thomas Tallmadge, in his *Architecture in Old Chicago*, gives the true meaning of the city's glorious new creations:

. . . they present a distinct bracket in architectural design in which the men of the eighties in presenting the steel skeleton to the world clothed it in a dress they thought appropriate and which came near to being indigenous. . . . It must be remembered that all of these

giants were built in a period of élan, almost all by young men, fired with a conviction that Chicago was the wonder-city of the world and bolstered up in the idea by the amazement of Europe and by the grudging admiration of New York.

It is not surprising that it was a Chicago writer, Henry B. Fuller, who became the first American novelist to take for his subject the life of the great industrial city. The opening of his appropriately named *The Cliff-Dwellers* is an evocation of the world of the skyscraper:

Between the former site of old Fort Dearborn and the present site of our newest Board of Trade there lies a restricted yet tumultuous territory through which, during the course of the last fifty years, the rushing streams of commerce have worn many a deep and rugged chasm. . . . Each of these cañons is closed in by a long frontage of towering cliffs, and these soaring walls of brick and limestone and granite rise higher and higher with each succeeding year, according as the work of erosion at their bases goes onward. . . . Ten years ago the most rushing and irrepressible of the tor-rents which devastate Chicago had not worn its bed to a greater depth than that indicated by seven . . . "stories." This depth has since increased to eight — to ten — to fourteen — to sixteen, until some of the leading avenues of activity promise soon to become little more than mere obscure trails half lost between the bases of perpendicular precipices.

A new architecture had been born, an architecture without fluted columns or the white statues of long-dead gods, an architecture voicing Lincoln's dream of a nation without master or slave. Louis Sullivan summed up its creed in his *Kindergarten Chats:*

Bank upon democracy, for your country is as surely and will remain surely a democracy, as it is sure that the sun will rise and set. Do not give yourself a moment's worriment about this. And arrange your architecture for Democracy, not for Imperialism. . . .

In its flowering, the Chicago School did indeed arrange its architecture for democracy. But in the wings the forces of imperialism were rapidly gathering strength.

Toward the Stars

In the last quarter of the nineteenth century, Chicago felt that it was destined to give expression to a new, wholly American, civilization. Boston was entangled in memories of England, New York but a monument to Mammon, and the South a wreck in the wake of the Civil War. In Abraham Lincoln the city had already given the Republic a new political being; its writers, such as Theodore Dreiser, were trying to fashion a revolutionary, realistic approach to literature; and its builders were prepared to turn away from the past and strike out for a native architecture. Studying the structures they had already produced by the early 1890s, the French novelist Paul Bourget quickly grasped their meaning: "It is the first draught of a new sort of art — an art of democracy . . ."

MONUMENTS ALONG THE LAKE

If any one building may be said to have begun the new art, it was Burnham and Root's Montauk (*left*) built in 1882 on West Monroe Street and first rented to the Hartford Insurance Company. The architectural historian Thomas Tallmadge asserted that "what Chartres was to the Gothic Cathedral the Montauk Block was to the high commercial building." Casting aside classical columns and Victorian furbelows, its young designers raised a straightforward structure of brick, relieved only by bands of terra cotta. The Montauk was destroyed in 1902 and replaced by the First National Bank Building.

What the Montauk was to the history of design, William Le Baron Jenney's Home Insurance Building of 1884 (*above*) was to the history of construction. It was the world's first iron-and-steel-framed building. The Home Insurance, which stood on the corner of La Salle and Adams Streets, was demolished in 1931.

One of the earliest examples of the Romanesque style, which formed the basis of so much Chicago School design, was Solon S. Beman's brick and granite Pullman Building of 1883 (*left*). Its arched entrance (*below*) was particularly admired. Standing at the corner of Michigan Avenue and Adams Street, the structure contained, in addition to offices, the Tip Top Inn, favored by Anna Held and George M. Cohan, as well as luxurious apartments, whose residents included Florenz Ziegfeld, Jr. The building was demolished in 1956.

"Four-square and brown, it stands, in physical fact, a monument to trade, to the organized commercial spirit, to the power and progress of the age, to the strength and resources of individuality and force of character . . ."
— Louis Sullivan, *Kindergarten Chats*.

Henry Hobson Richardson's Marshall Field Wholesale Store of 1885 (*above*), was one of the few buildings to which Sullivan ever gave an unqualified accolade. He was not alone; the Bostonian was one of the few eastern architects unreservedly admired by the men of the Chicago School. Still four-square, filling the entire block bounded by Adams, Quincy, Wells, and Franklin Streets, Richardson's Romanesque masterpiece was casually destroyed in 1930.

The effect of Richardson's Marshall Field Store is readily observable in Adler and Sullivan's Walker Warehouse of 1888 (*above*), originally built for Martin Ryerson, Jr. *Below:* The building's imaginative decoration, which would become a Louis Sullivan trademark. This aesthetically historical structure, which stood on Wacker Drive, was obliterated in 1953.

THE AUDITORIUM

A view north on Michigan Avenue in 1889, with Adler and Sullivan's Auditorium
Building under construction on the left. On the right is the Exposition Building,
designed in 1873 by William Boyington and built to proclaim Chicago's recovery
from the fire. In the Exposition Building, James Garfield was nominated for Presi-
dent in 1880, and Grover Cleveland in 1884. Afterward it was the setting for the
Theodore Thomas concerts which revealed such a vast audience for serious music in
Chicago that their chief backer, Ferdinand Peck, commissioned the Auditorium.
The Exposition Building was razed in 1891 to make way for the present Art Institute.

135

The Auditorium, with its luxurious hotel accommodations, public rooms, and opera house, was an outstanding example of how a single structure can enhance urban life.

Left: Visitors on top of the Auditorium Tower in the 1890s when it was the destination of all who wished to view the wonders of the prairie metropolis.

Below: The Michigan Avenue entrance to the 400-room Auditorium Hotel. It was on the balcony above that Hobart Chatfield-Taylor, in his book *Chicago,* reported hearing Sarah Bernhardt proclaim that the city was "the pulse of America."

The observation deck is now closed, and the Auditorium Hotel was a victim of the Depression.

Above: The long bar of the Auditorium Building, whose decoration gave Louis Sullivan the right to be called one of the creators of Art Nouveau. In a staggering act of vandalism, when the Congress Street Expressway was built in the early 1950s, 16 feet were sliced off the Auditorium's first floor and this seminal room was one of the casualties.

The Auditorium's 175-foot long main dining room (*left*) and its 4000-seat opera house (*below*) were superb examples of Sullivan's love affair with the arch, expressed in his *Kindergarten Chats:* "It is a form so much against Fate, that Fate, as we say, ever most relentlessly seeks its destruction. Yet does it rise in power so graciously, floating through the air from abutment to abutment, that it seems ever, to me, a symbol and epitome of our own ephemeral span." To emphasize his beloved arches, Sullivan, in this the world's first fully wired new building, made brilliant use of electric lighting.

During the first two decades of this century, when opera flourished in Chicago and Mary Garden enraptured audiences in *Pelléas et Mélisande,* the house was filled with Chicago society. After Samuel Insull built his gargantuan Civic Opera House in the 1920s, the grand old theatre was abandoned by Chicago's music world and fell into decay. It is now slowly being restored. The dining room, no longer serving its original function, is presently part of Roosevelt University, which occupies the hotel section of the building.

THE STOCK EXCHANGE

Another Adler and Sullivan landmark was the Chicago
Stock Exchange on the corner of La Salle and Washington
Streets, seen here (*above*) shortly after its completion in
1894. The special glory of the Exchange was its iron work,
for Sullivan, like most Art Nouveau designers, was fascinated
by the medium. *Right:* An elevator-cage door.

Left: A stairway with decoration reminiscent of Sullivan's French contemporary, Hector Guimard, who designed the Paris Métro stations. Though the Stock Exchange was listed by the Landmarks Commission as one of the most significant structures in Chicago, it was destroyed in 1972. *Above:* The powerful façade shortly before razing. This view was taken by the Chicago photographer Richard Nickel, who lost his life during the building's demolition.

SKYSCRAPERS

"These great Olympian buildings strike me as having beauty of a very high order," the British painter John Lavery told Harriet Monroe in 1911, after looking at Chicago's skyscrapers. "There has been nothing on earth like it since Egypt built the pyramids."

One of the earliest of the Olympians was the Tacoma (*left*), on the northeast corner of La Salle and Madison Streets, completed in 1889 from designs by Martin Roche and engineering by his partner, William Holabird. The Tacoma was the first building constructed by using rivets, the first whose architecture openly revealed the steel structure beneath, the first to inch toward the concept of the all-glass wall. This Olympian was demolished in 1929.

Among John Wellborn Root's last designs was the splendid headquarters for Frances Willard's Woman's Christian Temperance Union (*right*). For this building, constructed in 1892, on the southeast corner of La Salle and Monroe Streets, Root turned away from the more virile Romanesque style and found his inspiration in the châteaux of France's Loire Valley. Ironically, the Woman's Temple was demolished in 1926 when the organization it housed was at the height of its power.

143 - Chicago Womans Temple
J. W. Taylor Pho.

Not all of the city's skyscrapers followed the aesthetic precepts of the Chicago School. Two of the more notable mavericks are shown here. The Columbus Memorial Building on State Street (*left*) was an 1893 creation of the still-vigorous William Boyington. It possessed in the statue of Columbus over the entrance, in its elevator grilles and other fittings, some of the city's finest bronze work. The flamboyant relic of the Exposition years was torn down in 1959.

There was a time when few Americans would not have recognized the building on the right as "The Busy Beehive" headquarters of Montgomery Ward. The distinctive Italian Renaissance skyscraper on Michigan Avenue — the tallest in the world when it opened in 1900 — was designed by Richard E. Schmidt, one of the city's most prolific twentieth-century architects. (J. Massey Rhind's twice life-sized statue of Progress on top was said by Louis Sullivan to resemble a lady in her bath.) The building no longer houses Montgomery Ward's offices; its pyramid roof has been removed and Progress is no more.

Burnham and Root's Masonic Temple of 1890–1892 was among the handsomest Chicago School skyscrapers and also one of the most famous. "There was also the Masonic Temple of twenty-one stories, at the time the tallest building in the world, from the top of which . . . one could see Council Bluffs, Iowa, 230 miles distant," Edgar Lee Masters wrote in his memoirs. "I had to try that out, and Uncle Henry took me to the Masonic Temple." The building performed an extremely important aesthetic and urban function in Chicago, standing as it did at the corner of State and Randolph Streets, the crossing of the city's Rialto and its retail center. Its thoughtless demolition in 1939 and its replacement by low, undistinguished commercial structures left a large rent in Chicago's fabric.

With its crisp lines, light piers, and large windows, Holabird and Roche's Republic Building on State Street marked the last stage in the development of the tall commercial building of the Chicago School. It was originally 12 stories high when it opened in 1905, but in 1909 it was raised to 19. Still structurally sound and financially viable, the Republic was demolished in 1961 to make way for the Home Federal Savings and Loan Association Building.

The dazzling White City of the 1893 Columbian Exposition astonished both America and the world. This view shows Frederick MacMonnies' elaborate fountain on the right, and, on the left, the Roman-style Agriculture Building by McKim, Mead and White.

VIII

Dreams of Empire

As THE FOUR HUNDREDTH ANNIVERSARY of Columbus' discovery of the New World approached, the federal government announced that there would be a national exposition to commemorate the event. America's cities entered the competition like thoroughbreds at the Derby. New York, Washington, St. Louis, as well as Chicago, were all strong contenders. But Chicago worked hardest and it had impressive credentials. Since the fire, it had passed both Philadelphia and Brooklyn to become the nation's second largest city and its citizens were convinced that in ten years it would take first place. Mayor Carter Henry Harrison saw the fair as the crowning achievement of his colorful five-term reign, and he soon had a committee of three hundred working to bring the Columbian Exposition to the shores of Lake Michigan. To show just how determined it was, by 1890 Chicago had issued stock worth $5 million to begin construction. These efforts were only spurred on by the snide comments of the eastern press, which predicted that if Chicago got

the Exposition it would be a cattle show. When Charles A. Dana, editor of the New York *Sun*, pontificated: "Don't pay any attention to the nonsensical claims of that Windy City," Chicagoans seized the appellation and made it their own. All the hard work paid off when, on April 21, 1890, Congress designated the Windy City as the fair's official site.

One of the reasons for the selection of Chicago was the fame of its architects. The fair, it was assumed, would provide a spectacular show place for this exciting native American school. The assumption was proven correct when Daniel Burnham and John Root were appointed its architectural directors, for all America knew them as the men who had built the Rookery and the Monadnock.

Before a single structure could be raised, there was the all-important matter of location. Within the city an intense rivalry broke out between the North, West, and South sides; and Chicago turned for guidance to the greatest landscape architect of the day, Frederick

Law Olmsted, the creator of New York's Central Park. Olmsted was no stranger to Chicago. In 1868 he had, to the west of the city, laid out the town of Riverside, whose well-planned greenswards and winding tree-lined streets became a model for garden suburbs across the country. Afterward, the South Park Commissioners had retained Olmsted and his partner, Calvert Vaux, to furnish plans for the improvement of Chicago's recreational facilities. The result was the most complete and elaborate scheme adopted by an American city until that time. Olmsted called for a ring of parks around Chicago, a kind of green belt, connected by broad, tree-screened boulevards. In time, these parks — Washington, Garfield, Jackson — would become the pride of the city and one of its most profoundly civilizing influences. Here it was possible for urban workers to have an occasional green thought in a green shade.

Olmsted and his young assistant, Henry Sargent Codman, eventually settled on Jackson Park on the South Side. It was undeveloped — a mixture of swamp, sand, and scrubby trees — but it had two significant advantages: it was easily accessible to the heart of the city and it lay along the lake. The latter was extremely important, for Olmsted and Codman felt that an international exposition honoring Christopher Columbus must have water as its central element. Now, at the very beginning, they made possible that shimmering assemblage of formal pools, canals, and lagoons, which, more than any other single factor, was to make the Columbian Exposition memorable.

Meanwhile, Root had found a worthy architectural model for Chicago. The nation's last fair, the Philadelphia Centennial Exposition of 1876, had become a byword for tasteless vulgarity. But in 1889 France had astonished the world with its *Exposition Universelle*. Root went to Paris to study the Exposition in detail and returned filled with admiration for the daring 360-foot span of Ferdinand Dutert's iron-and-glass Galerie des Machines and for its centerpiece, Gustave Eiffel's elegant, soaring 1000-foot tower. Chicago's fair, too, would display modern technology with style and panache. As Root's sister-in-law, the poet Harriet Monroe, wrote in her biography of him:

. . . it should be a great, joyous, luxuriant midsummer efflorescence, born to bloom for an hour and perish — a splendid buoyant thing, flaunting its gay colors between the shifting blues of sky and lake exultantly, prodigally.

It would, in essence, be a reflection of the Chicago School and of the vibrant city that had nurtured it.

Though Root felt that the fair should be, above all, an expression of the heartland, he believed just as strongly that architects from other sections of the country should participate. In line with this he sent out invitations to Richard M. Hunt, to McKim, Mead and White, and to George B. Post, all of New York; to Peabody and Stearns of Boston; as well as to Van Brunt and Howe of Kansas City. Following guidelines set down by Root, these architects would be allowed to design a circle of buildings around the Court of Honor. All the fair's other structures would be allocated to Chicagoans.

Ever since he had begun his task, John Root had driven himself at a terrible pace. Not only had he been traveling almost constantly, drawing and redrawing plans, speaking to business and civic groups, and personally guiding important visitors over the fair's bleak, windswept site, but he had been attempting to carry on the work of his own busy office. He was, in fact, exhausted. Just as all of his efforts were beginning to bear fruit, on the very day the architects of the fair were to meet, John Root became ill. That night his ailment was diagnosed as pneumonia, and four days later, on January 15, 1891, he was dead. Root had been the ideal spokesman for the inland architects; more than any other man, he possessed a true vision of what a fair held in Chicago should be. Harriet Monroe expressed his hopes:

He wished to offer to the older nations a proof of new forces, new ideals, not yet developed and completed, but full of power and prophetic charm. He wished to express our militant democracy as he felt it, pausing after victory for a song of triumph before taking up its onward march.

Now there would be no proof of new forces, no expression of democracy. After Root's death, Daniel Burnham assumed command, and Burnham was a man without feeling for such ideals. As he told Louis Sullivan, this was a time "to work up a big business, to handle big things, deal with big businessmen." Sullivan had been shocked by these words, but Burnham, like a hound sniffing the air, had caught the correct scent. The egalitarian age of Lincoln had been succeeded by the era of the trusts, whose monopolies in sugar, oil, steel, coal, beef, and even ice created two

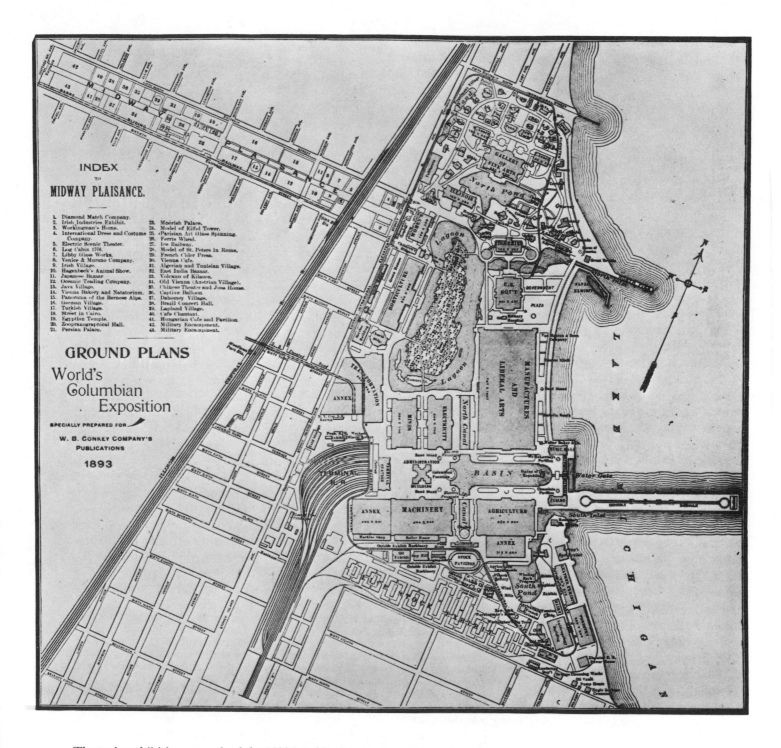

INDEX

TO

MIDWAY PLAISANCE.

1. Diamond Match Company.
2. Irish Industries Exhibit.
3. Workingman's Home.
4. International Dress and Costume Company.
5. Electric Scenic Theater.
6. Log Cabin 1776.
7. Libby Glass Works.
8. Venice & Murano Company.
9. Irish Village.
10. Hagenbeck's Animal Show.
11. Japanese Bazaar.
12. Oceanic Trading Company.
13. Java Village.
14. Vienna Bakery and Natatorium.
15. Panorama of the Bernese Alps.
16. German Village.
17. Turkish Village.
18. Street in Cairo.
19. Egyptian Temple.
20. Zoopraxographical Hall.
21. Persian Palace.

23. Moorish Palace.
24. Model of Eiffel Tower.
25. Parisian Art Glass Spinning.
26. Ferris Wheel.
27. Ice Railway.
28. Model of St. Peters in Rome.
29. French Cider Press.
30. Vienna Cafe.
31. Algerian and Tunisian Village.
32. East India Bazaar.
33. Volcano of Kilauea.
34. Old Vienna (Austrian Village).
35. Chinese Theatre and Joss House.
36. Captive Balloon.
37. Dahomey Village.
38. Brazil Concert Hall.
39. Lapland Village.
40. Cafe Chantant.
41. Hungarian Cafe and Pavilion.
42. Military Encampment.
43. Military Encampment.

GROUND PLANS

World's
Columbian
Exposition

SPECIALLY PREPARED FOR

W. B. CONKEY COMPANY'S
PUBLICATIONS

1893

The main exhibition grounds of the 1893 World's Fair covered the area from Lake
Michigan to Cottage Grove Avenue and from 56th Street to 67th Street. The site is
now Jackson Park. The Midway Plaisance was the Fair's amusement section,
reserved for such attractions as the exotic dancer Little Egypt and the giant Ferris
Wheel. It later became the location of the University of Chicago.

nations within the republic, one of capitalists and one of workers. Burnham was aware that Chicago itself had ceased to resist the long arm of eastern monopoly. A Philadelphian, Charles Tyson Yerkes, with the backing of the traction magnate, Peter A. B. Widener, had taken over the city's streetcar system. In 1889 the important grain elevator company of Munger, Wheeler had been bought by an English syndicate. More and more New Yorkers and New Englanders sat on the boards of Chicago's banks and owned its choice real estate; the latter development was vividly illustrated in 1890 when Hetty Green, "the witch of Wall Street," opened an office in the city. But nothing so starkly revealed the change as the sale of that quintessential Chicago institution, the grand old Union Stock Yards, to a New Jersey corporation. The Yards' new president was no Morris or Armour or Swift, but Mr. Nathaniel Thayer of Boston, Massachusetts.

Now the fair would express this new reality. With a score of brilliant Chicago architects to choose from, Burnham passed over them all, and selected as Root's replacement Charles B. Atwood, a draftsman in the fashionable New York firm of Herter Brothers and a close friend of Richard Morris Hunt. If one had to choose a moment when the seed was planted which grew into Chicago's Second City complex, this is that moment. The fair, which was to proclaim to the world in blazing colors the ideals of the heartland metropolis, was transformed by that act into a gleaming white advertisement of eastern taste. Atwood himself built the Palace of Fine Arts; Hunt the Central Administration Building; McKim, Mead and White the Agricultural Pavilion; Peabody and Stearns the Machinery Hall; Van Brunt and Howe the Electricity Building; George B. Post the thirty-acre Manufactures and Liberal Arts Building. Executed in the best Beaux Arts manner, the edifices resembled the confections of a pastry cook rather than serious architecture. Over their iron-and-steel frames was poured staff — a mixture of plaster of Paris and hemp fibers — and over that was sprayed a coat of dead-white paint. As a final flourish the *palazzi* were sprinkled with garlands and statues. So many craftsmen were needed to give everything just the right pseudo-classical cast that the sculptor Augustus Saint-Gaudens seized Daniel Burnham and cried, "Look here, old fellow, do you realize that this is the greatest meeting of artists since the fifteenth century?" A close look at Frederick MacMonnies' fountain, which one wag said resembled nothing so much as eight parlor-maids attempting desperately to sweep the water out of the lagoon while their mistress sat imperiously above them on a precariously placed chair, might make one question Saint-Gauden's enthusiasm, but he undoubtedly sounded convincing to Burnham.

There were two structures that broke the Fair's Beaux Arts pattern. Henry Ives Cobb, who had built a castle for Potter Palmer on Lake Shore Drive, designed an imaginative assemblage of circular pavilions containing aquariums and angling displays for the fisheries exhibit. And Adler and Sullivan made the centerpiece of their exotic Transportation Building a bright, welcoming door of carved arabesques sheathed in silver and gold. It alone was true to Root's dream, the one "joyous, luxuriant midsummer efflorescence" in the White City.

Nevertheless, the Columbian Exposition was a titanic achievement for a municipality which had been pronounced dead scarcely twenty years before. Chicago had every reason to be proud when, on May 1, 1893, Grover Cleveland — in the presence of Mayor Harrison, the Infanta Eulalia representing the successors of Ferdinand and Isabella, the Duke of Veragua who claimed descent from the Discoverer himself, and an assembled throng of about one million — officially opened the fair. As the President touched a golden telegraph key, ten thousand electric lights flashed on, the sprays of a dozen fountains shot into the air, a hundred flags unfurled, Theodore Thomas' orchestra struck up the "Columbian March," and over on the Midway the giant Ferris Wheel, the first in America, and Little Egypt simultaneously began their gyrations. In a country where few had ever seen a finished town and almost none had beheld outdoor electric illumination, the White City seemed a miracle, a paradise complete.

Foreign visitors also were impressed. William Stead, the English editor of the influential *Review of Reviews*, whose book, *If Christ Came to Chicago!*, is one of the most interesting studies of the city of the '90s, began his four-month stay by going to the fair. His praise was unqualified:

Never before have I realized the effect which could be produced by architecture. The Court of Honour, with its palaces surrounding the great fountain, the slender columns of the peristyle . . . and the golden dome of the Administration Building, formed a picture the like of which the world has not seen before.

The fair brought people to Chicago from the far corners of the world. An Indian, Mulji Devji Vedant, writing in the *Asiatic Review*, was no less enthusiastic than Stead:

To me the World's Fair presented a spectacle that exceeded all my expectations of grandeur. The majestic White City where poverty has no place to live, exercises over the mind such a charm, that its defects, like the dark spots of the sun, are invisible to the naked eye, owing to the great halo of lustre that pervades throughout.

There was one man who saw the dark spots. Louis Sullivan, already an incipient alcoholic and more and more exhibiting those personality disturbances which, two years later, would lead to the disastrous dissolution of his partnership with Adler, saw the Columbian Exposition as the death knell of the democratic architecture he hoped for. In his *The Autobiography of an Idea*, he recalled:

These crowds were astonished. They beheld what was for them an amazing revelation of the architectural art, of which previously they in comparison had known nothing. To them it was a veritable Apocalypse, a message inspired from on high. Upon it their imagination shaped new ideals. They went away, spreading again over the land, returning to their homes, each one of them carrying in the soul the shadow of the white cloud . . . they departed joyously, carriers of contagion, unaware that what they had beheld and believed to be truth was to prove, in historic fact, an appalling calamity.

The millions who came to the fair would indeed carry the example of the White City across the land. It would be imitated in a thousand museums and libraries and court houses whose monumental stairways, gargantuan columns and echoing halls would be a sincere flattery to the shimmering mirage on the shores of Lake Michigan. For Sullivan, the compliment brought no joy. "The damage wrought by the World's Fair," he said prophetically, "will last for half a century."

The make-believe world of the Columbian Exposition ended even before the gates shut, for in the fair's final hours Mayor Harrison was assassinated by a de-mented job-seeker. The act heralded bad times to follow. The closing of the fair found the United States in the worst business depression of the nineteenth century, and Chicago, flooded with men who had flocked to the Columbian boomtown, was particularly hard hit. Hundreds slept in the corridors of the County Building; thousands were saved from starvation by the saloons' free lunches.

The city's workers were not prepared to accept the situation without protest. Chicago was the center of labor union organizing in the United States; a Chicago poem had become the anthem of the all-important Eight-Hour Day movement:

> *We mean to make things over, we are tired of*
> * toil for naught,*
> *With but bare enough to live upon, and ne'er*
> * an hour for thought;*
> *We want to feel the sunshine, and we want to*
> * smell the flowers,*
> *We are sure that God has willed it, and we*
> * mean to have eight hours.*

The first great confrontation had come in 1886 in Haymarket Square. An orderly meeting of workers, listening to speeches by anarchists and others protesting the shooting of six strikers who had demanded an eight-hour day from McCormick, was charged by a phalanx of 200 policemen. Someone — never identified — threw a bomb into the midst of the police. Instantly there was a barrage of pistol shots from both sides, killing outright one policeman and one civilian. Eventually, seven more officers died from their wounds. During the hysteria that followed, eight anarchist leaders were brought to trial and four were hanged on the tenuous charge of inciting to violence. Illinois's new Democratic governor, John Peter Altgeld, had just pardoned those anarchists still in prison in 1893 when he had to deal with a far greater conflict.

The worsening economic situation was being felt with appalling sharpness in George Pullman's model town. With the demand for railroad cars declining, Pullman had reduced his work force, shortened hours, and cut wages by 25 percent while refusing to lower rents in his company-owned houses. In 1894, his desperate employees joined Eugene Debs's American Railway Union and there soon followed a nationwide boycott in which railway workers refused to handle

Pullman cars. Pullman demanded that the Governor ask for federal troops to break the strike, but Altgeld replied that since there had been no violence he had no legal grounds for such a request. Pullman then appealed directly to President Grover Cleveland, and on July 2, 1894, Cleveland, swayed by arguments that the strike was affecting the United States Post Office and the federal courts, ordered the troops to Chicago. The Railway Union was temporarily smashed, Debs was arrested for conspiracy, and a young lawyer who stepped forward to defend him, Clarence Darrow, began his magnificent career on behalf of the poor, the oppressed, and the unpopular.

These sounds of distant battle rarely intruded into the drawing rooms of Chicago's millionaires, who now began living on such a scale that, for the next half century, "Chicago packing fortune" and "Chicago dry-goods fortune," became, in American and English fiction, literary shorthand for limitless wealth. Along Prairie Avenue on the South Side the very rich dwelt in a proximity the likes of which could be found only in the upper reaches of New York's Fifth Avenue. There, side by side, stood the mansions of George Pullman, Philip D. Armour, John J. Glessner of International Harvester, William B. Kimball of pianos, and Marshall Field, whose dwelling by Richard Morris Hunt was the first in the city to be electrically lit. Field's former partner, Levi Z. Leiter, gave society something to talk about in 1895 when his daughter, Mary Victoria, married George Nathaniel Curzon, Marquess of Kedleston and future viceroy of India. The bride's father sweetened the deal by presenting the happy couple with $700,000 in cash and a guaranteed annual income of $30,000. Field too could be magnificent on occasion, as when he threw a $75,000 costume ball for his son, Marshall Field, Jr., and his daughter Ethel. Gilbert and Sullivan's *Mikado* was very much the rage just then, and so everyone was asked to come *à la Orientale*. As a final fillip, Field had James McNeill Whistler design the party favors.

All the magnificence was not on the South Side. North of the Loop, near the old Water Tower, the real estate tycoons John V. and Charles B. Farwell lived in brotherly harmony next door to one another. Charles's mansion, by the firm of Treat and Foltz, was in the popular Queen Anne style and appropriately baronial as befitted a United States senator at whose table Generals Grant and Sheridan had dined. Charles's special passion was rare sixteenth-century

books, and his library contained one of the world's half dozen best collections. But when it came to books, Charles Farwell was no match for the Bordens farther north at the corner of Lake Shore Drive and Bellevue Place. The Bordens not only read books, they wrote them. William Borden, a lawyer and mining engineer who had made a fortune in the Leadville, Colorado, strike, had proclaimed his good luck by having Hunt run up for him an impressive limestone French château. His daughter Mary became a well-known novelist — *A Woman with White Eyes, Sarah Defiant, Flamingo;* his son John wrote about his Arctic Circle explorations; his second wife Courtney penned *Adventures in a Man's World;* while a granddaughter became a leading patron of *Poetry* magazine and the wife of America's most literate twentieth-century politician, Adlai Stevenson.

But if Chicago had a Buckingham Palace in these years it was without doubt the crenelated "Norman" castle Henry Ives Cobb and Charles Sumner Frost built at 1350 Lake Shore Drive. For here dwelt Chicago's queen, Bertha Honoré Palmer, intelligent, handsome, awesomely energetic. Arrayed in her famous pearls and wearing a diamond tiara, she seemed more regal than royalty, especially, Chicagoans noted, when, during the fair, she returned the haughty snubs of the Spanish Infanta with charm and good manners. Mrs. Palmer could, with equal ease, persuade Mary Cassatt to paint the murals for the Columbian Exposition's Woman's Building, handle real estate investments, and give dinner parties that delighted everyone from President McKinley to struggling artists. Artists were often invited to 1350, for art was Bertha Palmer's passion. The gallery of her castle glowed with more Impressionist paintings than any room in any other private house in the world. When she discovered that among the 600 works sent by the French government for display at the Palace of Art there was not a single Impressionist canvas, she corrected the oversight by loans from her own collection, so that the crowds at the Fair might see pictures by Renoir, Monet, Pissarro, Sisley, and Degas.

Mrs. Palmer's avant-garde taste in painting is indicative of the atmosphere of the city of the '90s. For the next two decades there would be scarcely a movement in architecture, literature, education, or social theory which did not have either its roots or its best expression in Chicago. Nowhere was this more evident than at the University of Chicago, which under the leadership of William Rainey Harper had been newly refounded on the fair's old midway. There in the '90s John Dewey was conducting classroom experiments and writing his epoch-making *The School and Society,* which would transform American education. There too, Thorstein Veblen was studying Chicago's rich and using his observations for *The Theory of the Leisure Class.*

The university, though, had no monopoly on the city's educational efforts. On Halsted Street on the West Side, Jane Addams had established her "Cathedral of Humanity," Hull House, the nation's pioneer settlement house. Here she and her fellow workers not only fed and clothed and counseled men, women, and children, but created a dynamic cultural center which they hoped would transform the lives of the inhabitants of the slums around them. Hull House's theatre reached such heights that William Butler Yeats went there to see his verse drama performed; its lecture series became the one platform in America where a Russian anarchist or a union leader or a suffragette could always get a hearing. It was at Hull House, too, that the concept of the university extension course was born, with law taught by Clarence Darrow, economics by Henry George, and architectural theory by Frank Lloyd Wright, who delivered there his seminal "The Art and Craft of the Machine."

The city's cultural ferment was also reflected in its 25 daily newspapers, whose staffs were the envy of editors across the country. None could match the glamour of the *Record,* with George Ade, whose witty "Stories of the Streets and of the Town," illustrated by the deft hand of John T. McCutcheon, proved him one of America's finest humorists, and Eugene Field who alternated between his "Sharps and Flats," one of the first newspaper columns, and his delightful children's poems: "Wynken, Blynken, and Nod" and "Little Boy Blue." *The Record*'s chief competitor for literary laurels was the *Evening Post.* The *Post* had the incomparable Finley Peter Dunne, "Mr. Dooley," who expressed the uncomplicated but profound wisdom of the Irish living "Back-of-the-Yards."

If the Windy City had a supreme voice in this decade, though, it belonged to a young man named Theodore Dreiser, who arrived from Indiana just as the '90s began. His recollection of the excitement he felt, expressed in *A Book about Myself,* strongly echoes Louis Sullivan:

It is given to some cities, as to some lands, to suggest romance, and to me Chicago did that hourly. It sang, I thought . . . and I was singing with it.

Dreiser also worked on a Chicago paper, the *Daily Globe.* His coverage of all aspects of urban life would surface again in the rich details of *Sister Carrie,* for that novel is, in fact, a kind of Baedeker of the metropolis of the '90s. On the train bringing Carrie Meeber to the capital of the Midwest, Drouet, the man who will initiate her into a new world, remarks, "Chicago is getting to be a great town . . . It's a wonder. You'll find lots to see here." For Dreiser, this was a rare case of understatement.

The Fairs

It is not surprising that the two most architecturally significant of America's fairs should have been held in Chicago, for, beyond all other American cities, Chicago has expressed its creative drive in buildings. The World's Columbian Exposition of 1893, organized to celebrate the four-hundredth anniversary of the discovery of the New World, marked the triumph in the United States of the Beaux Arts style, an architecture which found its inspiration in classical models, usually Italian or French. The Century of Progress, held in 1933 on the centennial of Chicago's incorporation as a town, just as clearly signaled the demise of that fashion and the advent of the modern, International style. Both fairs were a tribute to the vigor of the city in which they took place: the first, a wonderland created only two decades after the nation had questioned whether Chicago would rise again from the ashes of the Great Fire; the second, a brave show in the face of the Great Depression.

THE COLUMBIAN EXPOSITION—1893

Above: Princess Eulalia, the Infanta of Spain, representing the nation that sponsored Columbus' voyages, on the Midway with her escort. The pagodas are at the entrance to the Chinese theatre. *Left:* The 600-foot-long Corinthian Peristyle designed by Charles B. Atwood. Each column honored a state, while the triumphal arch in the center, which faced Lake Michigan, was dedicated to Christopher Columbus. *Overleaf:* Daniel Chester French's statue of the Republic gazes across Frederick Law Olmsted's Grand Basin toward Richard Morris Hunt's Administration Building. No one who saw this composition ever forgot it. Years later, Theodore Dreiser was to recall the "splendid Court of Honor, with its monumental stateliness and simple grandeur . . ."

The Exposition's official Beaux Arts style was deemed appropriate for any sort of display. *Above:* Behind its fanciful façade, William Le Baron Jenney's Horticultural Hall was an expression of the Major's continuing interest in engineering problems. The crystal dome of its central pavilion, which housed full-grown palms, tree ferns, and giant cacti, was 187 feet in diameter. *Right, above:* The Palace of Mechanic Arts by the Boston firm of Peabody and Stearns was advertised as being inspired by both the monuments of Paris and the domes and towers of Renaissance Spain. *Right, below:* A structure more interesting for its architect than for its architecture was the arcaded 400-foot-long Woman's Building by Sophia Hayden. The inspiration of Mrs. Potter Palmer, the building not only was designed by a female, but featured exclusively displays of work by women. There were labor-saving devices for women such as the first gas range, and it was decorated with murals by the painter Mary Cassatt.

The two structures that dissented from the Columbian Exposition's classical canon were Adler and Sullivan's Transportation Building (*left, above*) and Henry Ives Cobb's Romanesque-inspired Fisheries Building (*left, below*). In the midst of the White City, Sullivan's gold-leafed entrance was a blazing spark of life.

Above: The entertainment sensation of the fair was the enormous Ferris Wheel, the world's first, designed by George Washington Ferris. Each compartment held forty passengers, and one was usually reserved for a band which played, time and again, the Exposition's hit song, "After the Ball Is Over." After the fair was over, the Ferris Wheel was moved to North Clark Street, remaining there until 1904, when it was taken to St. Louis to delight visitors at the Louisiana Purchase Exposition.

CENTURY OF PROGRESS—1933

"The individual who goes to A Century of Progress Exposition hoping to walk in
the midst of what he might look upon as classic splendor," Franklin Booth wrote in
a brochure on the architecture of the fair, "will not find the thing that he hopes for."
Below: The Hall of Science, where the Century of Progress' central theme, applied
science, was illustrated with imaginative exhibits, including one on atomic energy.
The Hall was the work of Paul Cret, the Philadelphian responsible for Washington's
Folger Shakespeare Library. *Right:* One of the two towers of the Sky Ride, the
Century of Progress' answer to the Columbian Exposition's Ferris Wheel. In front of
it is the Federal Building, the collaboration of Arthur Brown of Los Angeles and
Edward Bennett of Chicago, which struck a note often seen in the architecture of
the fair, part pared-down modern, part Hollywood.

164

The Century of Progress introduced Americans to the work of a large number of modern sculptors, including Lee Lawrie, Carl Milles, Gaston Lachaise, and Ernst Barlach. *Left:* The entrance to the Electrical Building's Social Science section, decorated with Leo Friedlander's sculptured pylons representing fire, light, darkness, and water. The building itself was designed by Raymond Hood, who had been responsible for the Chicago *Tribune* Tower. *Below:* The fair's symbol, Science Advancing Mankind, by Louise Lentz Woodruff.

The Travel and Transportation Building was the joint effort of the Exposition's architectural commissioners, including Hubert and Daniel Burnham, Jr., sons of the man most responsible for the Beaux Arts cast of the 1893 fair. The pavilion featured a structurally innovative suspended roof, the work of Holabird and Root.

Left: The Communications section of Raymond Hood's Electrical Building, an early example of modern windowless architecture. *Below:* The Owen Illinois House, which did much to create the '30s fad for glass-block construction.

Right, above: Buckminster Fuller's Dymaxion car, the three wheels and rear engine of which were supposed to revolutionize automobile design. *Right, below:* The Time and Fortune Building, showing the "Man of the Year."

Frank Lloyd Wright's Midway Gardens, which opened in August 1914 on Cottage
Grove Avenue near the University of Chicago, was a handsome illustration of
that "cleanly strength" the architect had called for in his famed Hull House lecture,
"The Art and Craft of the Machine." The Midway, whose winter garden is
shown here, symbolized in its combination of avant-garde architecture, good music,
food and drink, the urbanity of Chicago on the eve of the First World War. Among
the musicians who, in the 1920s, made the Midway a place of pilgrimage for devotees of jazz were the legendary "Bix" Beiderbecke and a young Chicagoan who
played there in 1924, Benny Goodman. After being used as a garage and car wash,
the Midway Gardens was destroyed in 1929.

IX

Where Is Athens Now?

At the beginning of the new century, Hamlin Garland, who would lovingly celebrate the heartland in *A Son of the Middle Border,* journeyed from Chicago, where he was living, to New York. There he saw powerful forces at work:

On my return to New York City in January, 1900, I found it in the midst of rebuilding, and I soon discovered that changes in the literary and artistic world were keeping pace with the swift transformations of the business world. New publishing houses were being established and new magazines . . . The esthetic life of all America was centralizing, with appalling rapidity, on this small island . . . The inland writer, like the inland publisher, was persuaded that in order to gain a national reputation he must speak from Manhattan.

Chicago's industry was being quickly linked to the East with golden chains, its architecture had already been dealt a fatal blow by the Atlantic coast's Beaux Artistes, and now the conqueror was laying claim to new territory. But it would take twenty years for the imperial triumph to be completed. In the meantime the Windy City would treat itself to two glorious decades.

By the end of the '90s Chicago's architects had mastered all the nuances of the Beaux Arts style, and, in some ways, had surpassed their teachers. Louis Sullivan had good reason to wonder why the bankers did not wear togas. On the site of the old Grand Pacific Hotel, D. H. Burnham and Company, as Burnham and Root was now called, constructed for the Illinois Trust and Savings Bank one of the world's most spectacular money-changing halls. Behind its 100-foot-long façade adorned with 36-foot monolithic Corinthian granite columns, the Illinois's vast banking room reveled in Siena violet, Alps green, and Numidian red marbles, as well as gold leaf, stained glass, and bronze. In 1905, Burnham sought to surpass this tour de force with his First National Bank Building. The First National consumed not only tons of sumptuous varicolored stone from Europe and Africa, but 150 railroad cars of pure white Vermont marble as well.

The businessman who cashed his checks and signed his notes amidst such grandeur obviously expected no less when it came to the essentials of food and shelter. Two hotels soon catered to this taste: the 1000-room La Salle of 1908 by Holabird and Roche, and the 500-room Blackstone, built two years later by Marshall and Fox. The first, in the very heart of the Board of Trade district, was constructed in the Louis XIV style, because, as a brochure said, "of the French associations of La Salle," a theme reiterated time and again by the architects' liberal use of the arms of the Sun King and the explorer. The La Salle's Blue Fountain Room became one of the city's most popular after-theatre rendezvous; if the play was boring, one could always count on a lift from the Blue Fountain's famed Tango-Banjo Orchestra. On Michigan Avenue near the Congress Hotel and the Auditorium, the Blackstone not only attracted a clientele of successful bankers and lawyers, but also from its opening day became the preferred locale for Chicago debutante parties. Famed for its food — after World War I it scored a coup by obtaining Kaiser Wilhelm's chief steward as its maître d'hotel — the Blackstone offered diners a choice of the airy Orangerie, the smart Café, or the regal dining room where, gazing out over the lake, one could savor champagne and blinis Romanoff.

The city's theatres were also affected by the new taste, which seemed to approve only of architecture suggestive of the French court. And in the infancy of the twentieth century, Chicago was an important theatre town, a close second to New York when it came to knowledgeable audiences, elaborate productions, and luxurious playhouses. As the center of the show-business "wheels" that brought drama and variety to the middle third of the nation, it is estimated that there were no less than 10,000 theatre people living in Chicago. When not on the road, they found ready employment in stock companies such as the Dearborn, one of the country's best; at theatres such as the Colonial, with its changing headliners like Eddie Cantor; at the Studebaker where George Ade's plays, *The Fair Co-ed,* starring Elsie Janis, and *Peggy from Paris,* premièred; at Charles Frohman's Grand Opera House with its presentations of Mrs. Fiske in *Becky Sharp* and George Arliss in *Disraeli;* at the Blackstone, where Mrs. Patrick Campbell captured the city's lasting affection by her performance in George Bernard Shaw's *Pygmalion.* Eleonora Duse had also accomplished that feat when, standing alone on the Auditorium's mammoth stage, she whispered the lines of her lover, the poet D'Annunzio. But there was one actress whom the city's playgoers cherished above all others. Sarah Bernhardt had won their undying devotion one night in 1891, when, after a performance of *Jeanne d'Arc,* she told the assembled reporters, "Chicago is the pulse of America." In the new century, when she played *L'Aiglon* at the Majestic, a sixty-year-old woman in the role of Napoleon's teenage son, the crowds filled the theatre night after night just to hear the timbre of her magnificent voice.

A dozen new theatres were built in downtown Chicago in these years. Among the handsomest was the Princess on Clark Street which reminded English visitors of London's Haymarket. The grandest of all, though, was the Illinois on Jackson Boulevard, which opened in January 1900, with Julia Marlowe in Clyde Fitch's patriotic drama, *Barbara Frietchie.* The work of the firm of Wilson and Marshall, the Illinois, with its limestone and granite exterior and a lobby of white Carrara marble set off by turquoise mosaics, was the epitome of the Beaux Arts style. Its rose, ivory, and gold auditorium featured a proscenium arch of genuine mother-of-pearl, and carried through the theme of the theatre's name by having four grand boxes each honoring one of the state's most famous sons: Stephen A. Douglas, Union generals Ulysses S. Grant and John A. Logan, and — some thought this a bit insensitive — Abraham Lincoln.

Chicagoans desiring a residence in the new fashion could be certain of unfailing good taste from David Adler. Of all the city's architects who wandered down the picturesque and eclectic Beaux Arts byways, he was one of the most interesting. No relation to Dankmar, David Adler, upon graduation from Princeton, followed the prescribed architectural course in Paris and, after he came to Chicago in 1911, produced an *oeuvre* of striking houses in Georgian, American Colonial, French and Italian Renaissance styles. His first commission, for an uncle, D. A. Stonehill, resulted in an impressive mansion in the Louis XIII manner on the lakeshore in Glencoe, north of the city. Over the next two decades, Adler was architect to some of Chicago's most prestigious names: Stanley Field, Albert Lasker, William McCormick Blair, Robert Mandel, and Richard T. Crane. None of his houses surpassed the Louis XIV style *hôtel particulière* he designed for Mr. and Mrs. Joseph Ryerson on Astor Street. A perfectly scaled building, it was often paid the supreme compliment of having visitors ask from what Paris mansion its *boiseries* had come. They had been carved in Chicago.

Yet the city's most spectacular twentieth-century Beaux Arts gesture was not a building at all. Still enamored with the White City's formal grandeur, Daniel Burnham had, in 1895, begun drawing up a vast scheme which would transfer the concept of the fair to Chicago itself. Using a phrase popular with Beaux Arts planners, Burnham called his idea "The City Beautiful," and was soon showing his drawings to any civic and business group willing to look. By 1902 his determination had reached such a height that he added a young man to his staff, Edward H. Bennett, whose chief task was to think up refinements for what Burnham had now officially labeled the "Chicago Plan." Daniel Burnham was an authentic genius when it came to public relations, and by 1907 he had pursuaded the powerful Chicago Commercial Club combined with the Merchants Club to assume sponsorship. Now, with the backing of the city's most influential business leaders, Burnham's dream began to become reality.

The essential vision of Burnham's City Beautiful is revealed in the credo he reiterated time and again: "Make no little plans. They have no magic to stir men's blood." One charge which could never be leveled against Daniel Burnham was that his plan was little. Like all Beaux Arts devotees, Burnham was enthralled by the procession of parks and open spaces — the Tuileries, the Place de la Concorde, the Champs Elysées leading up to the Arc de Triomphe — in the heart of Paris. He hoped to approximate it on the lakefront with a series of grand plazas, formal parterres, and triumphal gateways, but, like most American followers of the Beaux Arts, he envisioned everything on a superhuman scale. He failed to perceive that the Seine, which borders one side of the Tuileries gardens and the Place de la Concorde, is a narrow river and that the gardens are broader in appearance than in actuality. A park more than three times the width of the Tuileries edged by a huge lake might provide some spectacular vistas, but it was scarcely an inviting prospect for the casual stroller.

If giantism was Burnham's first sin, his second was an insensitivity to the importance of people to a city. Once again this was the result of a failure of perception. Burnham longed to emulate the grand boulevards which Haussmann had cut through the old city of Paris. But Burnham did not understand that above their first floor shops most of the buildings lining Haussmann's boulevards contained apartments, and behind them was densely populated medieval Paris. In the evening, on holidays, the people of Paris became *boulevardiers*, using the broad thoroughfares as urban parks, to window shop, to chat, to stroll, or from the table of a café to enjoy the greatest city pleasure of all, watching the passing show. In contrast, when Burnham turned to the creation of his boulevards he envisioned them lined almost exclusively with commercial and civic structures. Indeed his plan helped empty the Loop of people. The delightful Water Street Market along the river, Chicago's equivalent of Paris' Les Halles, was demolished to make way for the double-decked Wacker Drive. Thousands were evicted for the widening of Twelfth and other streets. In many ways, Burnham was the precursor of New York's highway-obsessed Robert Moses, as is revealed in this proud account by his friend and biographer, Charles Moore, of what the Chicago Plan had accomplished in its first ten years:

Of the improvements made in accordance with his plan, Mr. Burnham saw only the beginnings of the widening of Michigan Avenue . . . During the past decade Roosevelt Road (Twelfth Street) has been widened for a distance of two miles . . . A new diagonal, known as Ogden Avenue, is being cut from Ashland Avenue to Lincoln Park . . . The congested market area along Water Street is being reconstructed . . . and bond issues for the widening of Western and Ashland Avenues and Robey Street at a cost of seventeen and a half millions have been voted . . . The three outer highway circuits and their connecting radials as recommended by the Plan are complete . . .

No wonder the cry went up that the Chicago Plan was in reality a scheme to tax the poor to pay for the improvements desired by the rich. No wonder one of Burnham's legacies to Chicago was a Loop almost deserted at night.

Though the twentieth century witnessed the triumph of the Beaux Arts style, the Chicago School of Architecture did not expire at once. Its dying was to take fifteen years and those years were to encompass some of its finest achievements. At the very beginning of the century, Louis Sullivan received one of his most important commissions, a building on State Street for the Schlesinger and Mayer Department Store, a firm later purchased by Carson, Pirie, Scott. With its upper floors revealing, in their pure cellular outline, the realities of the building's form, and Sullivan's vigorous Art Nouveau decoration which framed the display windows, pointing up its function, the store was a structure of surpassing beauty.

One reason for the splendid execution of the Schlesinger and Mayer decoration was the sure hand of Sullivan's chief designer, George Grant Elmslie, who in 1909 resigned to become a founding partner in the firm of Purcell, Feick and Elmslie. Its first important Chicago commission came in 1912 when it was asked to design a shop and sales office for the Edison Phonograph Company. The result — a combination of crisp brick work, handsome terra-cotta decoration, and broad recessed panes of glass — was one of the most advanced and attractive small buildings of its day. It would be well into the '20s before shops of comparable design were built elsewhere.

Two other disciples of Sullivan, Frank Lloyd Wright and George W. Maher, were building during this period striking, innovative houses. Maher, who had come to Chicago in the 1870s, and who had worked with Wright and Elmslie in the 1880s, was a leading member of the Chicago Arts and Crafts Society, which encouraged fresh approaches to all aspects of design — furniture, stained glass, and fabrics, as well as architecture. In 1901 he designed for James A. Patten in Evanston an enormous granite house which, with its massive solidity, helped inaugurate a style which swept across the Midwest.

These were also the years when Wright designed some of his most accomplished "prairie houses," so-called because they were constructed for the heartland of materials that allowed them to fit easily into the landscape. These were houses for civilized citizens of a republic, houses whose open plan emphasized the informality of the New World, houses with furniture of their own time, houses where Wright substituted the word "playroom" for "music room" because they were not chambers for concerts by visiting artists but rooms in which a family could make music together. The mature period of the prairie house began in 1902, and after that Wright launched his structures like the perfectly crafted ships they so often resembled, their names being identification enough: the Heurtley, the Coonley, the Willitts, the Cheney, the Robie.

In 1913 Wright was asked to design a complex that in many ways symbolized the high level of urban life that existed in Chicago just before the First World War. The Midway Gardens, a pleasure ground near the University, was one of the Chicago School's most spectacular accomplishments, combining an open air café, a band shell, and a large winter garden, all decorated with tradition-shattering Cubist sculptures. The caliber of entertainment at the Midway Gardens was high indeed: a sixty-man symphony orchestra under Theodore Thomas' associate Max Bendix, guest performers such as the Russian ballerina Anna Pavlova, and, in the winter garden, one of the city's leading dance bands. There was superb food prepared under the direction of John Vogelsang, whose restaurant on Madison Street had been celebrated by Eugene Field, a marvelous wine cellar, and no less than six brands of imported German beer. The Midway was a delightful expression of the Chicago School's commitment to public architecture for public pleasure. Henry-Russell Hitchcock states in his study, *In the Nature of Materials,* the essential intention of the Gardens' architect:

Here Wright . . . aimed at public instead of private luxury, but not at the stodgy splendours of contemporary urban hotels and restaurants. Instead he sought a festive gaiety . . . a fresh open fantasia.

How well he succeeded is attested to by Edna Ferber, who used the Midway as a setting for her novel, *The Girls:*

It was deliciously cool there in that great unroofed space. There was even a breeze, miraculously caught within the four walls of the Garden. They ordered iced drinks. There was a revue between the general dancing numbers . . . A row of slim trees showed a fairy frieze above the tiled balcony.

The Midway Gardens was just one of the places in which to find the writers who now sprouted in Chicago with the astonishing swiftness of skyscrapers in the '90s. Another spot was Maurice's on West Madison Street, affectionately mentioned by John Gunther in his first novel, *The Red Pavilion*. There was the Tip Top Inn atop the Pullman Building on Michigan Avenue whose seafood dishes were a weakness of Floyd Dell's; the literary editor of the *Evening Post*, Dell would create a sensation in 1920 with his novel, *Moon-Calf*. The granddaddy of literary meeting places, however, was Schlogl's *weinstube* on North Wells Street. At its famed round table gathered the men who were giving America a new voice: Sherwood Anderson, Carl Sandburg, Robert Herrick, Edgar Lee Masters, Ben Hecht, Ring Lardner. So numerous did writers become in Chicago during these years that H. L. Mencken felt the city had annexed to itself the whole field of American letters:

In Chicago there is the mysterious something that makes for individuality, personality, charm; in Chicago a spirit broods upon the face of the waters. Find a writer who is undubitably an American in every pulse-beat, an American who has something new and peculiarly American to say and who says it in an unmistakably American way, and nine times out of ten you will find that he has some sort of connection with the gargantuan abattoir by Lake Michigan — that he was bred there, or got his start there, or passed through there in the days when he was young and tender.

Most of the writers earned their daily bread as newspaper reporters, though Masters was, briefly, Clarence Darrow's law partner and Sherwood Anderson wrote advertising copy. But their creative lives, almost without exception, circled around two remarkable, fully liberated women: Harriet Monroe and Margaret Anderson. From a distinguished Chicago family — her father had been a close friend of Senator Douglas — Harriet Monroe had, by the turn of the century, carved out for herself an impressive career. She had written an excellent biography of John Wellborn Root, worked as an art critic on the *Tribune*, and composed the official odes for the opening of both the Auditorium and the Columbian Exposition. Poetry, though, was always her first love, and now, determined that poets should have a proper publication in which to display their talents, she set

about raising money from people as diverse as Mrs. Potter Palmer and Samuel Insull, the utilities magnate, for a magazine which would print nothing but verse. The first issue of what she called simply *Poetry* appeared in October of 1912, and it soon numbered among its contributors William Butler Yeats, Rabindranath Tagore, and T. S. Eliot.

Harriet Monroe was particularly proud of *Poetry*'s encouragement of three poets from Illinois: Vachel Lindsay, Carl Sandburg, and Edgar Lee Masters. Lindsay's "The Congo" created a sensation with its pulsing rhythms which no one could render aloud better than the poet himself:

'Twas a land transfigured, 'twas a new creation.
Oh, a singing wind swept the negro nation . . .

Carl Sandburg's "Chicago" instantly became a kind of municipal anthem, the poem none dared omit when writing about the Windy City:

Hog Butcher for the World,
Tool Maker, Stacker of Wheat,
Player with Railroads and the Nation's Freight
    Handler;
Stormy, husky, brawling,
City of the Big Shoulders:

With *Spoon River Anthology*, Masters crafted the heartland's supreme epic, while his "Chicago" is a wonder-filled but subtle evocation:

Skyscrapers, helmeted, stand sentinel
Amid the obscuring fumes of coal and coke,
Raised by enchantment out of the sand and bog.
This sky-line, the Sierras of the lake . . .

Masters, Sandburg, and Lindsay also published in *The Little Review*, the magazine edited by the city's other phenomenal female. Beautiful and brilliant, Margaret Anderson had swept into town from Columbus, Indiana, in 1912, and Chicago was never quite the same again. The description of her reaction to the city in her autobiography, *My Thirty Years' War*, echoes the excitement felt by Dreiser and Sullivan:

Chicago: enchanted ground to me from the moment Lake Michigan entered the train windows. I would make my beautiful life here. A city without a lake wouldn't have done.

After a stint as a reviewer for the *Evening Post* and clerking in the bookshop Frank Lloyd Wright had designed in the Fine Arts Building — as the Studebaker Building was now called — Margaret Anderson decided that she would found a magazine which would, in her words, "make no compromise with public taste." She undoubtedly got some pointers from her boss, Francis Brown, who in the back room of his bookshop was editing the distinguished literary publication, *The Dial*. That Margaret Anderson meant what she said became evident when the first issue of *The Little Review* appeared in March of 1914. Pulling no punches, she came out strongly in support of Margaret Sanger and birth control and defended the well-known anarchist Emma Goldman. Her literary taste was equally as bold, and she broke new ground by publishing Ezra Pound, Hart Crane, and some of the short stories of Sherwood Anderson's *Winesburg, Ohio*.

It was a rare moment in Chicago. It would have been a rare moment in any city at any time. Sullivan and Wright had just completed two of the masterpieces of world architecture. *Poetry, The Little Review,* and *The Dial* were all being published there. In the Fine Arts Building, Maurice Browne was conducting the nation's first Little Theatre where it was possible to see the early efforts of Ben Hecht, Charles MacArthur, Sherwood Anderson, and Maxwell Bodenheim. Under Frederick Stock, the Chicago Symphony had reached new heights with more world premières than any other orchestra in America. Opera too was flourishing, spurred on by Chicago's own Mary Garden, who had created the role of Mélisande in Claude Debussy's *Pelléas et Mélisande*. Sitting in the Fine Arts Building with Henry Fuller, Hamlin Garland, and Garland's brother-in-law, the sculptor Lorado Taft, Henry James had, in 1905, expressed his surprise and approval. It was, he said, like the Paris of his youth. Now Masters, exploring the city with Sandburg, felt a new life in the air:

As I walked and went around with him I saw that there had come into being a Chicago of which I had but faint intimations. The town had studios where there were painters and sculptors, it had the precursors of the flappers, and here and there men and women were living together in freedom, just as they did in Paris. The year of 1914 was miraculous . . .

But then, at the very moment of its full flowering, Chicago began to wither; the vitality, which had first thrust it up through the black mud and then again through the charred rubble of its young dreams, began to fail. The First World War would be the killing frost, but before that, before Cantigny and Belleau Wood, the wild onion had turned sere. By 1915 there was a strange pervasive sense in the city that its one-time matchless vigor was dwindling, a feeling no doubt heightened by the awareness that hands so long at the helm were no longer there. George Pullman had died in 1897, P. D. Armour in 1901, Potter Palmer in 1902, Gustavus Swift in 1903, Marshall Field in 1906, Nelson Morris in 1907. One may not have liked them, indeed, may have hated them, but they could all say, as Norma Desmond did of the silent screen stars in *Sunset Boulevard*, ". . . we had faces!" The next generation could rarely make that statement.

Masters wrote:

> *This is a city of great doges hidden*
> *In guarded offices and country places.*

The country places were usually far to the north on the "Gold Coast," Lake Forest or Lake Bluff. The heart of old Chicago — Prairie and Indiana Avenues, Drexel and Grand Boulevards — was gradually abandoned. The new generation came into the city by day and fled again as night approached. In sharp contrast to the era when the oligarchy took a hand in running Chicago and put up mayors like William Ogden, John Wentworth, and Joseph Medill, the new style was to turn over the city's political life to the machine hacks. The mind of the new men is revealed by the story, most likely true, that Chicago was at this time offered the infant auto industry. After all, it was closer to the iron and coal, closer to the center of the country, than was Detroit. But its industrial barons said no. They didn't want the competition for workers from another giant. That is not the answer William Ogden or Potter Palmer would have given. The second-city virus had indeed triumphed. No one now spoke of Chicago's becoming America's first metropolis.

The changed atmosphere was felt most severely by the architects of the Chicago School. With the passing of the generation that had been willing to take a chance when Major Jenney said he could construct an iron-and-steel-framed building, the generation that had not flinched at the Montauk's unadorned façade or been shocked by Louis Sullivan's innovative decoration of the Auditorium, Chicago more often than not settled for uninspired, well-mannered imitations of East Coast design. Though Sullivan lived until 1924, the Schlesinger and Mayer Store was his last important Chicago work. For the next quarter-century he found his patrons in towns such as Owatonna, Minnesota, and Grinnell, Iowa. The Edison Shop brought Purcell, Feick, and Elmslie not a single serious Chicago job; Minneapolis was the beneficiary of the firm's discerning eye. George Maher was to die in obscurity in 1926, and after the Midway Gardens, Frank Lloyd Wright built in the West, in the South, in the East, and in Japan, but never again in the city that had first sheltered his genius.

The power of New York, which Hamlin Garland had perceived at the beginning of the century, now became irresistible to Chicago's writers. It was made even more so by the fact that the spacious days of the Chicago press were ended by the cut-throat competition brought on by the "yellow journalism" of William Randolph Hearst's *Evening American* and *Herald & Examiner*, which ultimately absorbed many of the fine old papers. The city exported its best. Dreiser had already gone. Hemingway, born in suburban Oak Park, wouldn't pause long enough to use Chicago as the setting for a single story. Gunther and

Ferber left; Sandburg and Masters; Floyd Dell and Ring Lardner. In 1917, Margaret Anderson decided that it was time to take *The Little Review* to New York:

I told everyone good-by — including the Fine Arts Building. I went to walk through its corridors which always seemed to me filled with flowers — its shops, which gave me the emotion of a perpetual Christmas.

Last of all I went to a symphony concert. Coming back to the Fine Arts Building I met Ben Hecht.

After you have gone, he announced, I'm going to have an electric sign put across the building:
WHERE IS ATHENS NOW?

Soon Hecht and MacArthur too would be in New York. Later, with *The Front Page*, they would preserve forever their Chicago salad days. In *Charlie*, his biography of MacArthur, Hecht remembered that his partner still pined for the Windy City, even though he was working for his old Chicago boss, the superb editor Walter Howey:

"You've got to love a town to be a reporter in it," MacArthur said to the persistent Howey, *"and baby, I don't love."*

"For God's sake," said Howey. *"Do you want to go back to Chicago?"*

"No," said MacArthur. *"That's over. But there's no place else."*

Places of Entertainment

"A year Carol spent in Chicago . . . She reveled in the Art Institute, in symphonies and violin recitals and chamber music, in the theater and classic dancing."—Sinclair Lewis, *Main Street*. An unfailing test of whether a city is truly alive is the quality of public entertainment it offers its inhabitants. The forms that entertainment might take are myriad: an evening of theatre or dancing, a well-served meal in an interesting atmosphere, a film viewed in an opulent auditorium. A vast complex of buildings and people may call itself a city, but without these places of public entertainment, it is but that, a mere complex of buildings and people.

THEATRES

Among the first to satisfy Chicago's craving for shows was James McVicker, who in 1857 built the $85,000 McVicker's Theatre (*below*) on Madison Street. After its destruction in the Great Fire, McVicker raised a grander theatre on the same site (*right, above*). It was in this house in 1881 that Sarah Bernhardt opened her first Chicago engagement with a repertoire that included *Phèdre* and *Camille*. McVicker's had another attraction: Gunther's (*right, below*), which served the best ice cream in town. Both the wonderful theatre and its luxuriant soda parlor are now only memories.

Left: The Divine Sarah in Chicago at the turn of the century. *Below:* Adler and Sullivan's first collaboration, the Central Music Hall, built in 1879 on the southeast corner of State and Randolph Streets. The upper floors housed the Chicago Musical College, presided over by Dr. Florenz Ziegfeld, father of the glorifier of the American girl. The building was demolished in 1900 to make way for the expansion of Marshall Field's Department Store.

Above: Randolph Street, Chicago's main theatre thoroughfare, in 1900. On the right are the columns of James J. Egan's City and County Building. Starting on the left are Powers' Theatre; the Sherman House, the city's favorite stopping place for show people; Burnham and Root's round-bayed Ashland Block, which housed the law firm whose members included Governor John Peter Altgeld, Clarence Darrow, and Edgar Lee Masters. Just visible beyond the Ashland Block is Adler and Sullivan's flat-topped Schiller Theatre Building, while in the distance is a pointed gable of the Masonic Temple, whose roof garden offered spectacular cabaret. All of these buildings have been razed.

Above: The Schiller Theatre Building of 1892 (later renamed the Garrick) was one of Adler and Sullivan's most pleasing achievements. The theatre proper occupied the structure's first seven floors and was proclaimed on the façade by a frieze of heads of famous composers and playwrights. The soaring tower contained offices, including the one where, in 1893, Frank Lloyd Wright began his private practice. *Right:* A Sullivan ornamental fantasy covering Dankmar Adler's superb shell which made the Schiller one of the country's acoustically finest houses. This gem of the city, a registered landmark, was destroyed in 1960 and replaced by a garage.

Two of the handsomest Beaux Arts theatres of the new century were the Illinois (*above*), on Jackson Boulevard between Michigan and Wabash Avenues, and the Princess (*right*), on Clark Street. The $250,000 Illinois, which opened in 1900 with the backing of the powerful producer-manager Charles Frohman, was the work of H. R. Wilson and Benjamin Marshall. Later, as the partner of Charles Fox, Marshall was responsible for the Blackstone and the Drake Hotels. The Illinois, the Chicago home of the Ziegfeld Follies, was replaced by a parking lot in 1936. The Princess, where the curtain first rose in 1906, was considered one of the city's best houses for straight drama, such as its 1914 hit, *Our Children,* starring Charles Ruggles. The building was designed by the Milwaukee architects Charles Kirchoff and T. L. Rose. In 1941, it too gave way to a parking lot.

DINING AND DANCING

Left, above: Love's on State Street, a pre-fire dining parlor offering both ice cream and oysters. *Left, below:* A State Street saloon, typical of those that got Chicagoans through cold winters and hot summers, with the alcohol lovingly analyzed by the city's own Finley Peter Dunne, better known as Mr. Dooley: " 'Tis a bad thing to stand on, a good thing to sleep on, a good thing to talk on, a bad thing to think on."

A food stand in Lincoln Park in 1902, a creation of a time when builders understood the necessity for fantasy in recreational structures and knew that inexpensive was not synonymous with mean.

1486

Chicago's large German population made a profound impact on the city's eating habits. Though Kinsley's on Adams Street (*left*) reveled in the Moorish façade F. L. Charnley gave it in 1885, the restaurant offered diners a popular German Room. A favorite meeting place of the city's architects, the room was the scene of much of the preliminary planning for the Columbian Exposition. Kinsley's was demolished in 1894.

Henrici's on Randolph Street (*above*) was, despite its Italian-sounding name, Chicago's pre-eminent German bakery-restaurant from the day it opened in 1875. It was the place where, late at night, one was most likely to see Lillian Russell, Ellen Terry, or other stars who were appearing at the nearby theatres. Henrici's lingered on until 1962.

One of the city's most romantic dining spots was the German Refectory in Jackson
Park (*above*), which had been the German Building at the Columbian Exposition.
The fairy-tale castle burned in 1925.

Chicago was indeed "that **toddling town**" and loved nothing better than a good dance band. Of them all, few could match King Oliver's Creole Jazz Band, shown above in Chicago in 1922. Its immortal members were, *left to right,* Johnny Dodds, Baby Dodds, Honoré Dutrey, Louis Armstrong, King Oliver, Lil Hardin (Mrs. Louis Armstrong), and Bill Johnson.

If Chicago had the best dance bands, it also had the best dance halls. *Left:* The $1,500,000 marble Trianon at 62nd Street and Cottage Grove Avenue, America's most luxurious public ballroom. The creation of Andrew and William Karzas, the Trianon opened in 1922 with music by Paul Whiteman and a grand march led by General John J. Pershing. The pleasure dome was demolished in 1967 to make way for an urban renewal project.

The Chez Paree, Chicago's supreme 1930s nightclub, at Fairbanks Court and Ontario Street. The building is now a warehouse.

MOVIE PALACES

In the '20s Chicago was, says Ben Hall, in *The Best Remaining Seats,* "the jumpingest movie city in the world and had more plush elegant theatres than anywhere else." The theatres were divided into two types, the "hard top" which traced its ancestry back to the European opera house, and the "atmospheric" which used lights to transform its ceiling into a sparkling night-time sky.

Right: The Paradise, on Crawford Avenue near Washington Boulevard, was the 1929 creation of Chicago's master of the atmospheric stars-and-clouds house, John Eberson. The Paradise was lost in 1956.

Left: The lobby of the Oriental, built on Randolph Street in 1926 by the city's other movie palace pioneers, Cornelius W. and George Rapp. Though the Oriental is still standing, it has been stripped of its extraordinary furnishings which made it, in the words of its builders, "a trip to the Orient."

BALABAN & KATZ
PARADISE
PARADISE
"WEARY RIVER" RICHARD BARTHELMESS BETTY COMPSON TALKING S
MARK FISHER "FLAPPER FOLLIES"-EVELYN WILSON PAUL KIRKLA
MUSICAL STAGE PRODUCTION "IL TROVATORE" MASSED CHORU
NEXT FRI. - MARY PICKFORD IN "COQUETT

Rapp and Rapp's elegant Norshore, which opened in 1926 on Howard Street to serve the affluent North Side, is recognized by movie palace buffs as one of the finest cinema theatres ever built. *Left:* The Norshore's outer lobby, crowned by crystal chandeliers suspended from a ceiling painted with Pompeian motifs. *Above:* The upper lobby, a conscious escalation of grandeur with gilded bronze, porcelain, and fine French antiques. *Right:* The theatre's richly decorated orchestra and loges. The Norshore was razed in the 1960s.

"He was on Cottage Grove . . . and before he knew it Mort
was up to Sixty-third, and saw the blaze of the Tivoli lights:
Constance Talmadge in *Wedding Bells*. The Tivoli was
supposed to make the Central Park look like a nickel show.
Those Balaban and Katz boys were certainly going strong."
— Meyer Levin, *The Old Bunch*.

The queen of the neighborhood houses that Rapp and Rapp built for the Balaban
and Katz chain was undoubtedly the South Side's Tivoli. *Left:* The solid marble
lobby modeled on Louis XIV's chapel at Versailles. *Above:* The theatre's vast seat-
ing. When the Tivoli opened in 1921 the legendary organist Jesse Crawford was at
the giant Wurlitzer. The theatre was torn down in the 1960s, a victim of television
and a changing neighborhood.

"They talked of how they would come home in glory and victory, marching down Michigan Boulevard with their medals and souvenirs." — James T. Farrell, *The Young Manhood of Studs Lonigan*. In this 1919 photograph, returning World War I soldiers parade along Michigan Avenue near the Art Institute.

X

Chicago Blues

THERE WERE TWO great cities that never fully recovered from World War I: Vienna and Chicago. Masters in his memoirs charged ". . . the World War destroyed the era out of which *Spoon River* came." Chicago had not wanted that war. Its foreign policy was well expressed by the noninterventionist position of Senator Robert La Follette from neighboring Wisconsin. It was a point of view shared by a broad spectrum of the city, from the Republican party and its spokesman the *Tribune*, through the German and Irish elements of the population, to humanitarians like Jane Addams, who headed the Women's International League for Peace, and the Socialists led by Eugene Debs. Chicago was dismayed by the vociferous bellicosity of its old Bull Moose hero, Theodore Roosevelt, laughed at the eastern socialites drilling at Plattsburgh, New York, distrusted the perpetual moralizing of the Princeton schoolmaster, Woodrow Wilson. Vachel Lindsay suggested in "Abraham Lin-

coln Walks at Midnight" that the war's legalized slaughter even aroused Illinois's supreme spirit:

It breaks his heart that kings must murder still,
That all his hours of travail here for men
Seem yet in vain. And who will bring white peace
That he may sleep upon his hill again?

The sanity of the heartland was not to prevail. While still piously protesting his reluctance to lead the United States into the conflict, Wilson merely waited for a chance to play a leading role on the world's stage. His task was made easier by German diplomatic ineptness, such as the famed Zimmermann note offering to help Mexico regain its lost territories in the American Southwest in return for an alliance with the Central Powers. There was also the matter of United States credits to the Allies. By 1916 these had reached the level where American banks suddenly held an astonishing one third of all the world's gold reserves. An Allied defeat, or even an indecisive resolution of the war, could have cost the country billions of dollars. Nineteen-sixteen was not a time to be sanguine about Allied prospects. It was the year in which the incompetent French general, Joseph Joffre, prepared the slaughter of half a million at Verdun, and Sir Douglas Haig, after announcing that the machine gun was a highly overrated weapon, sent 400,000 British to die at the Somme. While the Midwest spoke for neutrality, American intervention was demanded by Wall Street bankers like J. P. Morgan, industrialists like steel king Charles Schwab, by the New York press, and by the students of Harvard and Columbia.

Wilson had long been angered by the anti-interventionist stand of the heartland, and the Espionage Act, passed soon after America entered the war, gave him the weapon he needed to strike back. Its $10,000 fine and twenty-year jail sentence for disloyalty were ideal for silencing opposition. No midwestern city was more suspect than Chicago. With some 500,000 Germans in its population of two and a half million, it was, according to one official report, "the sixth largest German city in the world." Wilson's own statements against "hyphenated Americans" were soon echoed by his spy-hunting attorney general, A. Mitchell Palmer, who was capable of saying: "around sanger-fests and sangerbunds and organizations of that kind . . . the young Germans who come to America are taught to remember, first, the fatherland, and second America." Suddenly, singing Schubert became incompatible with patriotism. German clubs and music societies were closed, the German language forbidden in the Chicago public schools, and German newspapers placed under censorship. It was not a surprising development in an atmosphere which found pretzels banned because they had a German name and doctors striving to rechristen German measles. The effect on Chicago, however, was far from humorous. The German beer gardens and singing societies and the Turner Halls, with their active and independent political and intellectual life, had been among the most important influences in the city's neighborhoods. They had been civilizing centers, attracting not only Germans but Austrians, Scandinavians, Bohemians, and even the city's French, who were mostly from Alsace-Lorraine. Their disappearance extinguished lights in Chicago that were never to be relit.

The Germans were not Woodrow Wilson's only Chicago target. The city had for fifty years been the center of the nation's progressive political and social movements, and these too had no place in a country where every man, woman, and child was to be regimented into the war effort. The President, as the Chicago-born John Dos Passos observed in *Mr. Wilson's War*, ". . . saw Socialists, I.W.W.s [the Industrial Workers of the World], pacifists, anarchists of the Emma Goldman stripe all contributing in their separate ways to help enemy aliens and German agents impede the war effort." Wilson was quick to act. The Chicago leaders of the Non-Partisan League, which had backed La Follette, were arrested, Hull House was investigated, William D. Haywood and one hundred members of the I.W.W. were indicted by the city's federal district attorneys, and Eugene Debs was sentenced to ten years for sedition. Looking about him, Clarence Darrow came close to despairing of American liberties.

Washington's attack cut out the heart of political movements that traced their lineage back to some of Chicago's most sacred moments: the nomination of Lincoln, the Haymarket martyrdom, the battle for the eight-hour day, the struggle for child labor laws. Smeared as subversive, after the war they would never re-emerge with their former bright confidence. They would be labeled "foreign," "alien," when in fact they were one of the most American things about Chicago. Their disappearance as a force would be an important factor in turning the city over to the untender mercies of the political machine.

The pro-war forces had still one more terrible weapon to unleash on Chicago. For years the city had been the chief target of the Anti-Saloon League. The League spoke for America's small-town Protestants, for Baptists and Methodists, who saw in Chicago with its churches — Roman Catholic, Lutheran, Episcopalian, not to mention the synagogues, which used real wine in their sacraments, the depravity of Sodom and Gomorrah. The city was full of people who didn't speak English; it had beer halls; you could even get a drink on Sunday. New York was every bit as bad, but Chicago was closer to the League's strongholds. In the battle against drink, the war was a godsend. Now it was possible to argue that the use of grain to make alcohol was not only sinful, it was unpatriotic as well. Beer drinking, in particular, was anathema, for it was a German custom and it helped the brewers, who were almost all Germans. The Wisconsin superintendent of the Anti-Saloon League put the argument most succinctly:

Pro-Germanism is only the froth from the German beer-saloon. Our German Socialist party and the German-American Alliance are the spawn of the saloon. Kaiser kultur was raised on beer. Prohibition is the infallible submarine chaser we must launch by thousands.

Prohibition might be an effective submarine chaser, but in a city where more than half of the population paid a daily visit to a saloon it was difficult to enforce.

It did not take long for those willing to quench the city's thirst to get organized. By 1920 the now illegal breweries were producing at their pre-Eighteenth Amendment level, and beer-hustling was operating on a city-wide scale, with the business divided among rival gangs along lines that followed Chicago's natural divisions. In a matter of months Chicago became, in effect, a dozen states, each with its own military force. "Into the ranks of the several armies," reported Henry Justin Smith in *Chicago: The History of its Reputation*, "rushed practically all the clever or athletic young hoodlums 'educated' during the last twenty years." Now, in place of the friendly corner saloon, of the gracious ambiance created by John Vogelsang at the Midway Gardens and Joseph Schlogl in his North Wells Street *weinstube*, instead of the strains of Strauss and Lehar, Chicago got Big Jim Colosimo and Scarface Al Capone and the rattle of machine guns in the alleys of the North and West sides. George Ade was filled with nostalgia for *The Old-Time Saloon*:

During the nineties all of the alluring vices flaunted themselves in the open. Satan had all of his merchandise in the show-windows. The managers of the prolonged carnival did not kill one another. They cooperated, in the most friendly manner . . .

The friendliness had departed. Big Jim Colosimo was cut down in his café; Dion O'Banion shot in his flower shop; Hymie Weiss slain on the steps of Holy Name Cathedral; three of the six terrible Genna Brothers given, in the argot of the Chicago underworld, wooden overcoats. The stakes were enormous. The gang run by Johnny Torrio and Joseph Stenson

netted an estimated $50 million between 1920 and 1924, while the kingfish, Al Capone, was pulling down $100 million a year. Capone felt that he was performing a kind of altruistic service. "I make my money by supplying a public demand," he said. "If I break the law, my customers, who number hundreds of the best people in Chicago, are as guilty as I am. The only difference between us is that I sell and they buy." And if one was buying it was wise to buy from Capone. In his mock autobiography, *The Story of a Wonder Man*, Ring Lardner defined "a Chicago caddy" as "a boy who carries your ordnance bag, retrieves sliced or hooked bullets and replaces divots in bystanders."

As though struggling desperately to forget the mayhem, Chicago became in the '20s a city devoted to the architecture of fantasy. Two pastimes attracted its pre-eminent efforts: moviegoing and dancing. Chicago had always been a toddling town, but as the '20s began to roar, dancing became a craze. The new beat had begun in the winter of 1915–1916 when Joseph K. Gorham began bringing New Orleans jazz bands to the city. The new music was a hit, but Chicagoans, not certain what steps to do to it, at first just sat around and listened. One night at Lamb's Café, where a group called Brown's Band was playing, the manager announced that it was all right to dance to the new music. After this invitation, the onetime wallflowers threw themselves onto the floor with such gusto that Brown's Band remained at Lamb's for thirty-three thronged weeks. Henry Osgood, the pioneer writer in the field, claimed in *So This Is Jazz* that Chicago introduced the white world to the new music: ". . . the craze for jazz in the North and East appears to have come out of New Orleans via Chicago." Osgood was right; the Jazz Age was indeed born in the Windy City.

Chicagoans quickly adapted the New Orleans music to something highly acceptable to white dancers, and, as the '20s got under way, Chicago hotels were filled with the nation's best orchestras. Typical was Marshall and Fox's posh new $8,500,000 Drake at the spot where Michigan Avenue becomes Lake Shore Drive. The Drake's glittering Silver Forest, a vast room running the whole length of the hotel's north side, featured Fred Waring and Hal Kemp and first introduced Phil Spitalny and his All-Girl Orchestra. Chicago demanded the best. As the music historian James T. Maher points out:

Chicago was always a more sophisticated dancing city than New York. When Paul Whiteman was brought to Chicago with brassy fanfare the dancing Midwesterners turned their backs on his theatrical flair, his Wurlitzer-window display of instruments, and his symphonic arrangements.

Chicago's favorite dancing master was undoubtedly Isham Jones, an Ohioan who arrived in town just as the '20s began. In no time "Ish" was making the city sway to his brilliant saxophone- and piano-playing at the Old Green Mill. But he found his true home at the Sherman House's College Inn, run by Chicago's premier restaurant impresario Ernie Byfield, who claimed, among other things, to have invented the club sandwich. The Sherman, in the midst of the Randolph Street rialto, was the favorite hotel of visiting show people, and they soon spread the word about Jones's music. During the six years he stayed at the College Inn, Isham Jones created some of the most subtle dance music in America. Soon orchestras were not only imitating his style, but playing the songs he wrote: "Swinging Down the Lane," "It Had to Be You," and "I'll See You in My Dreams."

The musicians in Chicago's downtown hotels and clubs were all white. But a black note had been sounded in the city. The decade from 1910 to 1920 saw a wave of blacks sweep into town from the South, many of them to fill the jobs left vacant by whites going off to join the army. In that decade the city's black population doubled to more than 60,000. A bloody six-day race riot in the summer of 1919, that left 22 blacks and 16 whites dead and more than 500 people injured, did not discourage the new arrivals. Settling in the decayed grandeur of the South Side, they moved into houses vividly described in Richard Wright's *Native Son:* "That was the way most houses on the South Side were, ornate, old, stinking; homes once of rich white people, now inhabited by Negroes or standing dark and empty with yawning black windows."

The houses might be old and the winters cold, but life in Chicago's Black Belt was better than it was in Mississippi or Alabama or Louisiana. Lynching was not a regular diversion, there was work in the stock yards, and, between 47th and 48th Streets, the lights were always bright. So they came on the Illinois Central, the "Green Diamond" as it was called, to the very spot where Lincoln's body had been brought home, to the Twelfth Street Depot, which became a kind of black Ellis Island. Chicago was mid-America's black capital, what Harlem was for the East, celebrated in a thousand songs such as Little Brother Montgomery's "Lake Front Blues":

> *Chicago, Chicago, that is the town for me,*
> *Chicago, Chicago, that is the town for me,*
> *Drop me off by the lake front, that's where*
>   *I'll be contented to be.*

Now to the city that had welcomed McCormick and Pullman and Root and Dreiser came a black talent. Louis Armstrong arrived from Louisiana in the summer of 1921. He had been sent for by Joe "King" Oliver — who had created a sensation with his Creole Jazz Band at the Lincoln Gardens — to play cornet for an astounding thirty dollars a week. Armstrong had no hesitation about leaving New Orleans; he remembered the day of his departure as the greatest day of his life and wanted to shout to everyone he met that he was going to Chicago. Through the Romanesque arches of the old Illinois Central Station, Louis Armstrong, like thousands of other blacks, came to his new city. Robert Goffin, who worked closely with him on *Horn of Plenty,* described Armstrong's feelings this way:

The train arrived in Chicago at twilight of a blistering hot day. Louis was wearing his best black suit, his derby and a wing collar that was anything but spotless after the long trip. As he followed the hurrying crowd toward the nearest station exit, a sense of power surged in him . . .

The power was soon displayed at the Lincoln Gardens and the Royal Gardens and the Plantation Café, where Armstrong revealed to the world a new musical structure as astonishing in its way as the city's skyscrapers. Along with that architecture, this black jazz was America's only other original gift to the world's arts.

Places to dance were not limited to the city's hotels and clubs. In 1922, Andrew and William Karzas opened up a whole new concept with a $1,500,000 ballroom of marble columns, crystal chandeliers, and gilt which could trace its ancestry back to London's eighteenth-century pleasure grounds and the sumptuous dance halls of Second Empire Paris. Appropriately named the Trianon in honor of its Versailles-inspired splendor, it was, as the first-night program said, "truly a palace dedicated to dancing." Over the years the palace would make a place in the musical world for Ted Weems, Jan Garber, Kay Kyser, and the "Old Maestro," Ben Bernie. When, on February 18, 1923, Rudolph Valentino danced the tango at the Trianon, 6000 enthusiastic fans followed in his footsteps. The appearance of Valentino was prophetic. America's taste for fantasy was growing increasingly exotic, and when the Karzas brothers inaugurated a new ballroom in 1926 it was named the Aragon and was all Spanish-Moorish. There might be three feet of snow in the streets outside, but as the dancers whirled to the music of Wayne King or Dick Jurgens or Freddy Martin, inside it was Granada.

The architectural fantasy of the Trianon and the Aragon was surpassed only by the city's cinemas. Three men will always be associated with the Chicago movie theatre — Abe and Barney Balaban and Sam Katz. When Balaban and Katz decided in 1916 to build the Midwest's first motion picture palace, the 400-seat Central Park, they were fortunate in finding two architect brothers, Cornelius and George Rapp, who could give them exactly what they wanted. Along with Chicago's John Eberson, the master of the atmospheric stars-and-clouds house, and New York's John Lamb, Rapp and Rapp made up a triumvirate of sensational movie-theatre fabricators. But the Rapps were unequaled when it came to the presentation of stunning opulence without vulgarity. Among the dozens of Chicago theatres they built, two stand out as masterpieces of cinematographic architecture: the Tivoli on Cottage Grove Avenue, whose main lobby suggested the chapel Jules Hardouin Mansart had built for Louis XIV at Versailles, and the 3000-seat Norshore on Howard Street. The Norshore's restrained yet sumptuous Louis XVI interior was unquestionably one of America's finest classical compositions. It reminded theatregoers of the palaces of Paris and St. Petersburg, and in a 1925 interview George Rapp said that was exactly what he intended:

Watch the eyes of a child as it enters the portals of our great theatres and treads the pathway into fairyland. Watch the bright light in the eyes of the tired shopgirl who hurries noiselessly over carpets and sighs with satisfaction as she walks amid furnishings that once delighted the hearts of queens. See the toil-worn father whose dreams have never come true, and look inside his heart as he finds strength and rest within the theatre. There you have the answer to why motion picture theatres are so palatial.

In time, with their Paramounts in Brooklyn and Manhattan, the Rapps would show the East, too, how to build movie palaces. Not all of Chicago's architectural fantasy was in its ballrooms and cinemas. In 1921, on a spectacular site on Michigan Avenue just north of the Chicago River, the firm of Graham, Anderson, Probst and White had built for the Wrigley Chewing Gum Company a gleaming terra-cotta skyscraper ornamented with bits and pieces of Renaissance design. Floodlit at night, the Wrigley Building instantly became one of Chicago's most famous landmarks. Not to be outdone, in 1923 the *Tribune* announced an international design competition for its new home, to be constructed just across Michigan Avenue from the Wrigley Building. The commission's importance and the $10,000 prize attracted hundreds of entries from all over the world. The preliminary decision of the judges gave first place to the striking modern skyscraper designed by Finland's Eliel Saarinen, but the *Tribune*'s management reversed the decision and awarded the prize to New York's Raymond Hood and John Meade Howells. Louis Sullivan, old and ill and living almost forgotten in the back room of a cheap hotel, was astonished when Hood and Howells' structure turned out to be a Gothic tower replete with flying buttresses and niches for statues. "It is an imaginary structure — not imaginative," he wrote in *The Architectural Record*. Sullivan then went on to praise Saarinen's entry and to express his surprise that a foreigner had so perfectly captured what he considered to be the ideals of a true American architecture. Sullivan should not have been surprised, for his own work, and the work of Burnham and Root, of Holabird and Roche, and of Wright was known and admired by hundreds of contemporary European architects.

In a few short years, the leader of a new imperialism, Adolf Hitler, would arise in Germany to proclaim that "Never was humanity in its appearance and in its feelings closer to classical antiquity than today." Hitler would ban modern architecture, close schools such as the Bauhaus, which taught it, and ask his favorite architect, Albert Speer, to raise a becolumned Berlin. Then the ideals of Adler and Sullivan, of Root and Wright, cast out when Chicago itself had turned to its own brand of imperialism, would be carried back to the Lake Michigan shore by refugee architects such as Ludwig Mies van der Rohe. History, if it is anything, is convoluted and ironic.

Sullivan would not see that day. Within a year of the *Tribune* competition he died, possessing little more than a single suit of clothes and his drawing board, and was buried by the charity of a few faithful friends, including Frank Lloyd Wright, who remembered the heady days of the Auditorium. Until the very end, Sullivan had been working on *The Autobiography of an Idea*. Almost the last passage he wrote reaffirmed his faith in democracy and his belief that America would one day get the architecture it deserved: "That dream has never ceased. That faith has never wearied."

By the time Franklin Delano Roosevelt stood at the podium of the Chicago Stadium in 1932 and pledged a New Deal for the American people, none needed it more than the citizens of the Windy City. The prohibition wars had reached a climax in 1929 with the machine-gunning by Al Capone's boys of seven of rival George "Bugs" Moran's hoods in a North Clark Street garage. After that, St. Valentine's Day had a very special meaning in Chicago. The mobs had strong-armed their way into the city's cleaners and dyers trades, into the bakers and barbers, into the electrical workers and the garage repairmen, into the plumbers and the garbage haulers, the window cleaners, confectionery manufacturers, and the undertakers. The profits were estimated at $6 million a week. And nothing was done. Ferdinand Lundberg, a Chicago newspaperman in the '20s, who was later to write *The Rich and the Super-Rich*, remembered:

Nobody was ever convicted of murder in any of the gang wars that chalked up several thousand killed. Actually, all the gangs were politically connected and were paying off someone from the mayor down through the alderman, judges and others. Had the politicians wanted to squelch the gangs they could have easily done so. But the money lay in cooperating with them.

The 1929 Illinois Crime Survey reported that hoodlums had control of most of Chicago's voter lists and election boards. When Mayor "Big Bill" Thompson's safety deposit box was opened, it was rumored to have contained a million dollars in cash.

The stock-market crash left Chicago with an unemployment rate of more than 25 percent, a devastated banking system, and most of its hotels in receivership. This last was not a very serious matter for the hundreds sleeping under the Michigan Avenue bridge. Policemen and schoolteachers were paid in scrip, and in the Black Belt men didn't have the carfare to look for work. The disaster was compounded by the collapse of Samuel Insull's giant Commonwealth Edison Company which hit middle- and upper-income Chicagoans particularly hard. It was even difficult to escape the gloom momentarily, for Louis Armstrong and most of the city's best musicians had taken the train for New York.

As a final insult, desperate Chicagoans now meekly stood in line outside the kitchen Al Capone had set up near police headquarters. The sign read: "FREE SOUP, COFFEE, AND DOUGHNUTS FOR THE UNEMPLOYED." Indeed, Capone became a kind of local folk hero. After a visit to Chicago in 1930, the novelist Mary Borden reported in *Harper's* that he had pre-empted the conversation of a city which had once talked of Louis Sullivan and Theodore Dreiser and Jane Addams:

I went to a dinner dance . . . I met a lovely member of Chicago's four hundred who spoke to me with tears in her eyes of Capone. I was already getting rather sick of the Scarface, but this suddenly made me feel quite ill, this sentimentality frightened me.

It was a different town from the one that had gone wild at the announcement of the nomination of "Honest Abe."

Chicago made one gallant effort to dispel the gray clouds hanging over it. To celebrate the centennial of becoming a town, it staged in 1933 on the lakefront a Century of Progress Exposition. The fair's architecture, boldly modern, revealed a new wind blowing across America. Nowhere was this more startlingly shown than in the structures designed by Raymond Hood, who threw aside the Gothic trappings of his *Tribune* Tower for the sleek pared-down designs of the new International Style. The Century of Progress also broke ground with its lavish use of works by controversial modern sculptors such as Lee Lawrie, Gaston Lachaise, Leo Friedlander, Louise Lentz Woodruff, and Carl Milles. The fair's central theme, applied science, was brilliantly carried out, but its chief purpose, to attract some badly needed cash to the city, was not quite so successful. Sally Rand, the Century of Progress' answer to the Columbian Exposition's Little Egypt, reviewed the dismal results in an interview she gave Studs Terkel for *Hard Times: An Oral History of the Great Depression:*

They planned this Fair to bring business to Chicago, into the Loop. But you could have fired a cannon down State Street and hit nobody, because everybody was out at the Fair sleeping in their Fords.

The "Fords" were significant, for the infant industry which the city had once snubbed now came back to haunt it. From 3,000,000 in 1916, the number of automobiles had increased to 23,000,000 by the beginning of the '30s, or one for every five Americans. Combined with the more than 700,000 miles of surfaced roads in the country, the effect on Chicago was profound. Now the people in all the little towns in Iowa and Indiana and Wisconsin and Kansas could get into their cars or into a bus or a truck and drive straight to New York or California or Florida. The era of the portage and the canal had passed into history, and though trains such as the Twentieth Century Limited were reaching new heights of sophisticated design, the age of the iron horse was drawing to a close. Not a new mile of intercity track had been laid since 1920. All railroads led to Chicago, all roads did not. For the first time since its founding, the city was no longer the essential island, the natural capital of the heartland.

That is what it had been. Willa Cather's novel *Lucy Gayheart,* published in 1935, has for its heroine a girl from Nebraska who goes to Chicago to study music in the first years of the new century. There is a passage which celebrates her feeling for the city:

The next afternoon Lucy was walking slowly over toward Michigan Avenue. She had never loved the city so much; the city which gave one the freedom to spend one's youth as one pleased, to have one's secret, to choose one's master and serve him in one's own way. Yesterday's rain had left a bitter, springlike smell in the air; the vehemence that beat against her in the street and hummed above her had something a little wistful in it tonight, like a plaintive hand-organ tune. All the lovely things in the shop windows, the furs and jewels, roses and orchids, seemed to belong to her as she passed them. Not to have wrapped up and sent home, certainly; where would she put them? But they were hers to live among.

That was what Chicago had given the millions who had come to it, lovely things to live among: hotels and restaurants, ballrooms and theatres, department stores and parks, mansions and Pullman cars, concert halls and skyscrapers. For a hundred years the city had given and the gift had been glorious.

Lovely Things to Live Among

"God made the country," the English poet William Cowper wrote, "and man the town." Because the city is indeed man's handiwork, it is, at its best, one of the noblest expressions of the human spirit. One thinks immediately of Athens' Acropolis, Rome's Piazza Navona, and Paris' Place de la Concorde. But the creation does not have to be on such a grand scale. It can be a well-wrought shop front, a perfect tea house, an inspiring space, a lighted fountain. The one criterion is that it be, in Bernard Berenson's term, "life enhancing," something that lifts the heart and brings joy.

COMMERCIAL GRACE

Below: The elegant Victorian display windows of the State Street side of Marshall Field's Department Store, erected in 1878 and replaced by the present Field's building in 1907. *Right, above:* Daniel Burnham's classical Illinois Trust and Savings Bank interior in dazzling red, green, white, and purple marble. After the La Salle Street structure opened in 1897, Charles F. McKim wrote Burnham: "It will remain a monument long after you are gone." The banking temple did not long survive its architect and was demolished in 1924. *Right, below:* Spaulding's, a treasure house of diamonds, pearls, and gold-headed walking sticks, at State and Jackson Streets in the 1890s. The firm continues, but is now located in the Drake Hotel.

GARSON PIRIE SCOTT

Left: With unsurpassed assurance, Louis Sullivan's Schlesinger and Mayer Store (afterward Carson, Pirie, Scott and Company), begun in 1900, invited shoppers to view the delights within. Carl Condit, in his study *The Chicago School of Architecture,* called the building "... the ultimate achievement of the Chicago School and one of the great works of modern commercial architecture." The perfect composition of the State Street structure has been marred by the replacement of Sullivan's delicate cornice by a heavy, awkward parapet. *Right:* An example of how a small store front can help to humanize a busy city street. Purcell, Feick and Elmslie's Edison Phonograph Shop, built on Wabash Avenue in 1912, was, in its use of planting and in its open, welcoming entrance, one of the most advanced buildings of its time. It was cited in 1957 by the Commission on Chicago Landmarks as "a place of dignity and beauty." These qualities were evidently expendable: the Edison Shop was destroyed in 1967.

Chicago's tradition of carefully designed shop fronts continued through the 1920s and into the '30s. *Left:* The striking 1920s Art Deco façade of the Studebaker Service Building on the northeast corner of 26th Street and Michigan Avenue. Art Deco, which had a brief, vigorous vogue in the city, used decoration in a highly romantic way to celebrate the speed and movement of the new machine age. The Studebaker Service Building vanished in the mid 1960s. *Below:* Another Art Deco façade on the Palmolive Building on North Michigan Avenue. This splendid 1929 skyscraper was the result of the collaboration of John A. Holabird and John Wellborn Root, Jr. The fine metalwork has been altered to accord with the building's new function as a Playboy Club.

SPECIAL PLACES

Exotic flourishes are never more justified than when a structure attempts to whisk the viewer to a faraway place. *Above:* The White City amusement park on the South Side at 63rd Street and South Park Avenue presented its entertainments in an atmosphere reminiscent of Venice. Though it took its name from the Columbian Exposition, the complex was built after and totally separate from the 1893 fair. In the 1920s, its two dance halls reverberated with the music of outstanding Chicago jazz bands, such as the Wolverines with Jimmy McPartland. Near the end of the decade, White City was ravaged by a disastrous fire, and, in the early 1930s, the remnants of what was considered the country's finest Beaux Arts public amusement park were razed.

Left, above: The Hō-ō-den (Phoenix Hall), built by order of the Japanese Emperor for the Columbian Exposition, was one of this country's first examples of authentic Oriental architecture. Situated on the Wooded Isle in Jackson Park, the structure, known familiarly as the Japanese Tea House, continued to function as a charming refreshment spot until its demise during the Second World War. *Left, below:* The Italian Court on North Michigan Avenue, a 1921 transformation by architect Robert De Golyer of a group of undistinguished buildings. Irene Castle was a tenant of one of the Court's spacious studios, while Le Petit Gourmet, established by the widow of the Chicago poet, William Vaughn Moody, was the setting for readings by the contributors of *Poetry* magazine. The civilized little enclave was replaced by an office building in 1969. *Below:* The elaborate carousel of Riverview amusement park, Belmont and Western Avenues, was an adaptation of themes from Indian Mogul architecture. The cupola, for example, was inspired by the pavilions encircling the dome of the Taj Mahal, a likeness brought out at night when it was outlined in lights. Riverview, seen here in the 1920s, gave way to a housing development in the 1960s.

One of the most effective ways of making a city habitable is by the creation of a great enclosed public space. Among America's supreme interiors was the 300-foot-high octagonal rotunda of Henry Ives Cobb's Federal Building, completed in 1905. The rotunda, inspired by the monuments of Imperial Rome, was crowned by a dome 100 feet in diameter, larger than that of the Capitol in Washington. More than $2 million was spent on its polished granite, its white and Siena marble, its mosaics and gilded bronze. At the center of the composition, Cobb placed a *trompe-l'oeil* oculus or eye where white clouds perpetually drifted across an azure sky. (For an exterior view see page 9.) This unabashed expression of civic pride and Beaux Arts panache was destroyed in 1965–1966.

The architects of another of Chicago's exciting enclosed public spaces found their inspiration far from Imperial Rome. For the Diana Court in their Michigan Square Building of 1930, Holabird and Root looked to the Exposition Internationale des Arts Decoratifs held in Paris in 1925, from which came the term Art Deco. But their inspiration was even more specific, relating to the ocean liner design of the late 1920s and early 1930s, when the new *Ile de France* and *Normandie* made other ships seem old-fashioned and influenced land-based structures as well. There is about this room the sense of a grand salon on a transatlantic liner. The marble and bronze fountain that gave the court its name was by the Swedish sculptor Carl Milles. The Michigan Square Building and the subtle room over which the ancient huntress presided sailed into a cloud of wrecker's dust in 1973.

LIGHTS

The advent of outdoor electric lighting, first widely used at the Columbian Exposition, provided one of the most dramatic methods of enhancing urban life. The 1930s possessed a particularly sensitive feeling for this new medium. *Below:* The Fountain of Light at the 1933 Century of Progress, the creation of Joseph Urban, one of the period's best-known designers. *Right:* The Lindbergh Light atop the Palmolive Building, inaugurated shortly after the building's completion in 1930. With an intensity of 2 billion candlepower, it was the brightest beacon ever constructed and an imaginative tribute to the Lone Eagle.

Sweeping across the midwestern sky like a shimmering white finger, the beacon gave to downtown Chicago the excitement of a Hollywood opening. To all who came to the Windy City, by train or plane or automobile, it signaled that this was a place to be reckoned with, that here was power and pride, that here, in Willa Cather's phrase, were "lovely things . . . to live among." But in 1969 its 39-story pedestal was dwarfed by its new neighbor, the John Hancock Center. After that the Lindbergh Light no longer swept southward across the Loop and something precious disappeared. The nighttime sky was a bit darker, the city a bit lonelier; Chicago, in some inexplicable way, seemed suddenly to be lost.

SOURCES
AND NOTES

Sculptured decoration over the doorway of the 1908 Mary Crane Nursery of Jane Addams' Hull House. This photograph was taken March 31, 1963, the day before the property at Halstead and Polk Streets was turned over to the city for razing.

Sources and Notes for Illustrations

INDEX

Index